Your Towns and Cities in the Grea

Torquay
in the Great War

Your Towns and Cities in the Great War

Torquay
in the Great War

Alex Potter

Pen & Sword
MILITARY

Dedicated to the memory of the men of Torquay
who fought in and died in the Great War of 1914

First published in Great Britain in 2015 by
PEN & SWORD MILITARY
an imprint of
Pen and Sword Books Ltd
47 Church Street
Barnsley
South Yorkshire S70 2AS

Copyright © Alex Potter 2015

ISBN 978 1 47382 270 2

The right of Alex Potter to be identified as the author
of this work has been asserted by him in accordance with the
Copyright, Designs and Patents Act 1988.

A CIP record for this book is available from the British Library.

Printed and bound in England
by CPI Group (UK) Ltd, Croydon, CR0 4YY

Typeset in Times New Roman

Pen & Sword Books Ltd incorporates the imprints of
Pen & Sword Archaeology, Atlas, Aviation, Battleground, Discovery,
Family History, History, Maritime, Military, Naval, Politics, Railways,
Select, Social History, Transport, True Crime, and Claymore Press,
Frontline Books, Leo Cooper, Praetorian Press, Remember When,
Seaforth Publishing and Wharncliffe.
For a complete list of Pen and Sword titles please contact
Pen and Sword Books Limited
47 Church Street, Barnsley, South Yorkshire, S70 2AS, England
E-mail: enquiries@pen-and-sword.co.uk
Website: **www.pen-and-sword.co.uk**

Contents

Introduction and Acknowledgements

The First World War was the bloodiest war ever fought by the United Kingdom, costing the lives of around 723,000 men, and from mid-1917 onwards represented the only modern occasion when the British Army has taken the lead in a major land-based war. Since the advent of internet based family history, interest in the war has been steadily growing as online records have given people a tantalising glimpse into their ancestors' experiences of the war. As the historian Adrian Gregory reflected:

'The British seem to take the First World War personally. It would be difficult to imagine a contemporary British historian of the Napoleonic Wars writing a preface about how their great-great-great-grandfather died of typhoid at Walcheren or lost an arm at Badajoz, but it seems almost instinctive to evoke a grandfather at Loos or a great-uncle on the Somme.'

The author of this book is not immune. My great-great grandfather fought at Gallipoli and on the Western Front. My great-uncle served in the American Expeditionary Force and my great-grandfather enlisted at 15 and was discharged when his age was revealed. Every family has similar stories to tell but despite the growing public interest the war remains poorly understood. A war fought in appalling trench warfare conditions with huge casualty figures is hard to remember with anything but horror and what remains is a feeling of waste and blunder. However, this was not the unanimous view of those who fought; as many soldiers defended the war and their generals as lamented it as a great waste, and they fought it for a cause that many believed in.

The aim of this book is to tell the story of one small English town; to analyse its contribution to the war and its experience of the home front; to follow the social changes unleashed and to see how Torquay remembered the war. By doing so it hopes to present a more nuanced view than the mud and blood of popular imagination, while still acknowledging the horror and respecting the great suffering endured by the generation of 1914.

By featuring letters from serving Torquinians and following the career of Sir Herbert Plumer, commander of Second Army, who spent a substantial amount of his pre-military life growing up in Torquay, it aims to show that the British Army slowly forged the most effective fighting force of its era and ended the threat of Kaiserism to Western Europe.

Taking a cue from the style of Peter Hart *et al.*, extensive first-hand accounts have been used with the vast majority being letters from Torquinians unpublished since their appearance in local newspapers a century ago. Never has there been a better time to tell the story of Torquay's experience of the war than in the centenary year of its outbreak and I hope this book is up to even half the standards of those that gave their lives from 1914-1918.

A project of this size is never undertaken without the help of many others. My thanks go to the staff of Queen Mary University Library, the British Library, Torquay Library and Torquay Museum. Special thanks go to both Torquay institutions for their permission to reproduce the photographs within this book. Thanks go to Professor Dan Todman who, despite giving me my lowest mark in three years of university (!), fundamentally changed my view of the war, directly leading to this book; to Roni Wilkinson for commissioning this work and being an invaluable source of advice; to Tom Bradshaw, Rob Olford, Cody Strong, Blake Roberts and Ron Espino, without whom I would never have developed the historical ability to write this book; to Paul and Julie Fogarty for all their support; to Ashley Stalzer for offering assistance with data mapping and finally to Sabrina Link, without whom this book wouldn't exist. Two years ago I told her about my idea to write it and it was her support in the early days that has resulted in this book. She had the confidence in me and likewise I have the confidence that whatever she decides to do in life and wherever she goes she will succeed. Sabrina, consider this your dedication we talked about all those months ago. Not bad for a girl that can't pronounce Holborn and thinks the Wu Tang Clang terrorised the American South during the nineteenth century…If I have missed anyone my apologies, I'm sure I'll soon hear about it.

Chapter 1

1914 - Enthusiasm?

'England was at war. It had come. I can hardly express the difference between our feelings then and now. Now we might be horrified, perhaps surprised, but not really astonished that war should come, because we are all conscious that war does come; that it has come in the past and that, at any moment, it might come again. But in 1914 there had been no war for – how long? Fifty years – more?'

Agatha Christie

On 4 August 1914 Britain declared war upon Germany following its violation of Belgian neutrality. The myth of the war states that this news was met with a spontaneous outburst of jingoism but this was not the case; the reaction in Torquay is best summed up in Agatha Christie's quote above, a deep unease about the future.

In its first edition since the declaration, the *Torquay Times* published an editorial comparing what lay ahead to the effort required to win the Boer War, showing that the population were firmly aware of the facts rather than possessing a naive idea of war. On the same day a letter was published evoking the feelings of many, speaking of 'untold misery to the people concerned' and asking 'What does the present generation know of war?' Colonel Charles R. Burn, the town's Conservative MP, wrote to the Mayor, Charles Towell, preparing him:

'The die is cast and we must take our part in this terrible war. God knows it is not of our seeking; it has been forced upon us by Germany. That nation has flagrantly violated the rights of Belgium. . ..The call of honour and our own self-interest binds us to stand for the integrity of France, and thus we find ourselves drawn into this European Armageddon.'

These were not the reactions of a jingoistic population but of a concerned people thrust into the unknown. Anti-war sentiment was muted; while the Church of England immediately supported the war, the dissenting churches reacted with more reticence. Those in Torquay formed a group named the 'Free Churches of Torquay' (Belgrave Congregational Church, Upton Vale Baptist Church and Zion United Methodist Church) and sent a telegram to Prime Minister Asquith urging him to continue his efforts on behalf of peace, representing the most prominent anti-war action of the opening months.

Another documented incidence of anti-war sentiment occurred when someone circulated leaflets calling the declaration of war 'The Great Bluff!' stating, 'There will be no war' and signed by 'one who knows'. Aside from these events, there appears to have been a distinct lack of pacifism within Torquay despite the general anxiousness. Norman Cliff, a pre-war employee of the *Torquay Times* and the Torquinian that left the best record of service in the war reflected:

'As a small town youth nurtured in a puritan and conventional atmosphere, I had not encountered pacifist ideas or movements, and accepted without question the general attitude towards the armed forces, uniforms, patriotism, and the duty to defend one's country by fighting, and if necessary, by killing other young men who may seek to destroy it.'

Cliff's reaction was typical of the town, not an outpouring of belligerence but a more nuanced belief that one must do one's duty come what may, combined with a stoic appreciation of what lay ahead. The vicar of Upton Vale, the Reverend L.J. Roderick, summed this up stating that Britain was 'launching into a storm not to destroy but to save'. There was also little evidence of the 'over before Christmas' syndrome with an article in the *Torquay Times* citing the unknown duration of the coming war and attempting to analyse how long it might last, but concluding it was impossible to judge.

As Torquay came to terms with the idea of war, Mayor Towell was greatly concerned about the town's food supplies, keen to prevent any kind of profiteering. Despite his concern, the price of bread rose from 5½d the Saturday before the declaration to 6½d on 5 August. Towell was also worried about the impact upon Torquay's summer season and there was a heated discussion about whether to proceed with the Torquay Regatta, which, after great debate, was eventually cancelled due to a feeling that it was inappropriate. As the matter was under discussion, a great number of tourists scrambled to leave the town, increasing the feeling of anxiousness. Despite this general attitude, there were some spontaneous outbursts of patriotism. Visiting Breton 'Onion Lads' joined forces with local boys and marched along the Torbay Road singing the French and English anthems and there was a performance of the French and English national anthems at the Pavilion with the *Torquay Times* suggesting 'such a scene of enthusiasm has never been witnessed in the building'.

In the following days several hundred naval reservists left the town, witnessed by large numbers of residents who came out to wish them farewell, although the *Torquay Directory* (henceforth referred to as the *'Directory'*) reported that the march lacked the 'display of enthusiasm' on show across the bay at Brixham. With only the Boer War to compare with, some members of society also underestimated the situation while others were grasping the true reality. Both the *Torbay News* and the *Directory* argued:

'Something of the loss which has been inflicted upon Torquay's holiday season by the war will be recouped if there are efforts to boom the winter season. The chance is one which ought not to be missed. Traffic on the continent will be dislocated, if not impossible to any but combatants; and it is certain that few, if any, English people will be disposed to visit the usual Continental resorts...When France and Germany were at war in 1870 Torquay experienced what perhaps, was its most successful winter season...There must also be borne in mind the fact that in all probability many French people will visit England in the winter.'

While the potential for an increase in English tourists was debatable, reading this now it seems ridiculous anyone would even suggest that French tourists would visit while their country was being invaded.

The opening salvos of the war were now being fired and Torquay suffered its first casualty after only two days. Edwin Coombes, of Park Hill Road, married with two children, drowned on board HMS *Amphion* when she hit a mine on 6 August. *Amphion* was the first Royal Navy ship to be sunk and it was not surprising, given Torbay's naval tradition, that a Torquinian was amongst the casualties. It was seventeen days before the BEF's first major battle of the war but Torquay had already experienced its first death.

Attitudes towards the enemy in the first month were mixed. The *Torquay Times* proudly displayed an advert for 'Anglo-Bavarian Ale' below its masthead, apparently seeing little need to remove references to Germany. It also saw it fit to include a small article stating that a number of German waiters in the town had joined the German Army. The presence of those soldiers and that of Pierre Brottin, of the Torquay Municipal Orchestra, who left to join the French Army, emphasises how Torquay's experience of war wasn't limited to only those in the British forces.

Controversial stories about German conduct during the invasion of Belgium began to appear in the media within a few weeks and this started to change opinions. Twenty un-naturalised Germans were arrested and taken to Exeter, amongst them a man on his wedding day and a gentlemen who had lived in England for twenty years, married an English woman and 'was an Englishman by all his instincts'. As a sign of how unprepared the country was for war there was no provision for them and they were soon released back to Torquay on parole. At the same time Mr Basil Hindenburg, conductor of the orchestra, sensitive to the change in atmosphere, changed his surname to Cameron in an attempt prevent any confusion over his nationality. The Reverend J. T. Jacob, vicar of Torre, summed up the developing atmosphere:

> 'I am afraid of possible trouble that our own almost criminal leniency may bring upon us in England. No German can be looked upon as a friend, but ought to be looked upon as an enemy.'

The harmlessness of Torquay's German community was shown in the views of one of those arrested. The unnamed man had lived in Torquay for a number of years and was no fan of the war:

> 'The conditions are entirely different to 1870, which was to some extent at any rate aggressive on the part of France…In the present case Germany is, or rather the Kaiser, the aggressor. **** the Kaiser!'

The mass arrest failed to halt fears and a yacht was boarded as it sailed into the harbour due to concern that it was German; it turned out to be Spanish. A contributory factor to this outbreak of anti-German sentiment were rumours swirling around the town that an innocent meeting of the German Waiters' Association was a front for something suspicious. Tabloid newspapers had frequently printed invasion scare stories in the past such as William Le Queux's *The Invasion of 1910* featuring a fifth column of German spies infiltrating Britain and posing as waiters, clerks, barbers, bakers and servants. The parallels with Torquay's German community are obvious. Yet despite these events general attitudes towards Germany were fairly subdued during the opening weeks.

The declaration of war was quickly followed by Lord Kitchener's famous call for volunteers to enlist in the 'New Armies' which would expand the BEF from its small professional core. The first months saw the people of Torquay volunteering in disproportionately large numbers. The pre-war population of Devon numbered 669,550 of whom 38,771 lived in Torquay, but by mid-October 220 of the 1,200 men who had volunteered in Devon came from Torquay. Thus despite having only 5.15 per cent of Devon's population, Torquay contributed 18.3 per cent of its volunteers during the first two months. In part this can be attributed to socio-economics. Devon was a heavily agricultural county where many men did not enlist in order to bring in the harvest. In contrast Torquay's employment structure was based around transient service sector jobs and included a larger number of wealthy families. Despite this Torquay also had a strange demographic structure, including unusually large numbers of women and the retired. As such it can be confidently stated that during the opening stages of the war Torquay was contributing to the war effort far in excess of what was expected.

Kitchener believed that the war would be long and bloody and rejected proposals to distribute volunteers piecemeal throughout existing battalions. Instead he proposed the creation of New Armies, consisting of battalions of well-trained volunteers ready to be sent across the Channel in force the following year. Volunteers were organised into 'Service' battalions allocated to existing regiments, the Devonshire Regiment establishing the 8th, 9th, 10th and 11th battalions.

Regiments based in counties with small populations were always going to struggle to fill their ranks and thus it was quite common to see men from the larger industrial cities serving in regiments far from home. Although the 8th Devons were formed from a majority of Devonians, 9th Devons were far less Devonian in character with only about eighty Devonians in October. Despite this the newcomers were quickly taught the tradition of their new regiment and joined the natives in forming a strong *espirit de corps*.

In the major industrial cities 'Pals Battalions' of men who lived or worked together were formed to take advantage of their friendships. Torquay did not raise a Pals Battalion, its relatively small population and lack of any large-scale employers preventing a movement emerging. The closest Pals battalion was the 12th Gloucesters. Instead Torquinians mainly joined the Devons unless they stated a desire to enlist in another regiment.

Men enlisted for a diverse number of reasons. The historian Niall Ferguson suggested five factors for enlistment. The first was recruitment techniques such as the marching of military bands and newspaper appeals. These efforts were important in inspiring a patriotic spirit and were present in Torquay with the marches of the Breton Onion Lads and Torbay Boys on the first day and the appeals of the Torquay newspapers. Ferguson's second factor was female pressure; once again this was prominent in Torquay with a meeting of women at the Pavilion being the most visible example amongst other efforts including the display of a billboard with the slogan 'Wives, mothers, sisters, sweethearts...shame your men into joining'. However limits should be placed upon the strength of this factor; many women held their men back, worried about the health of their loved one and the previously mentioned billboard was much criticised. The third factor was peer pressure via institutions such as the Pals and sporting institutions. In Torquay this factor was weak due to the lack of a Pals Battalion and although there is evidence of a number of sportsmen volunteering, the sports clubs in the town were smaller and less influential than elsewhere.

His fourth factor is economic motives. In a tourist resort such as Torquay, the slump in the tourist industry caused by the war pushed some men into enlistment, others were blatantly coerced into volunteering by their employers, such as Norman Cliff who was sacked upon the declaration of war as an 'economy measure' and told that his place was in the Army. The Torquay Tramway Company also provided a large number of volunteers due to promising that their employees' jobs would be kept safe. Ferguson's final factor was 'impulse'; within this can be included concepts of adventure and a desire for new experiences. As with all young men this played a strong role amongst those bored of everyday life.

Ferguson is dismissive of the effects of patriotism and the Belgian factor, going as far as to state that in the majority of cases Belgium had little impact. In this regard his theory hardly fits Torquay. The local media was full of lurid accounts of German atrocities and from mid-September the town played host to a substantial population of Belgian refugees. The average Torquinian had ample opportunity to interact directly with Belgians and receive first-hand experience of their suffering. In a small town this would have happened frequently and had a large impact. Although a lesser influence in the opening month of the war, as the Belgian presence in Torquay increased, it played a more significant role in convincing men to enlist.

As for patriotism Ferguson suggests that those of the working class lacked the education that created the patriotic feelings of the middle class. Given Torquay's position as an unusually middle class town it could be suggested that its population would have been more educated and more patriotic than the average town of a similar size. Percy Fawcett, the famous Amazonian explorer and son of a middle class Torquay family, reflects this stating upon enlistment that he felt obliged 'by the patriotic desire of all able bodied men to squash the Teuton'.

The early enlistment phenomenon can only be explained by a combination of these factors. Recruitment techniques, the role of women, peer pressure, economic motives, impulse, patriotism and the treatment of Belgium combined to form the impetus to enlist. Amongst the middle class of the prestigious Warberries and Lincombes areas economic motives would have been less important and patriotic reasons stronger, while amongst the lower classes of Ellacombe the uncertain economic situation would have played a stronger role. The men who enlisted were of all social ranks and the men of Ellacombe and Pimlico stood side by side by the town's notables.

While Torquinians rushed to enlist, General Herbert Plumer was serving as General Officer Commanding-in-Chief for Northern Command and had now been placed in charge of the establishment of the first New Armies. Plumer had been born in London in 1857 but shortly thereafter his father had moved the family to live at Malpas Lodge, Torquay, where Plumer spent much of his childhood between Torquay and London before leaving for Eton and a military career. As such, despite his place of birth and his family's interests in London, Plumer grew up as much a Torquinian as a Londoner. He was a stereotypical figure, old, well rounded and with a large bushy white moustache, the very image of a blustering Colonel Blimp, however in the coming years he would prove to be anything but and would become one of Torquay's most prominent figures of the war

Alongside the volunteers many Torquinians were also serving in the Territorial Force and although they had signed up on the promise of only being used for home defence they were quickly asked to serve abroad. The 4th, 5th and 6th Devons all agreed. Kitchener had been dismissive of these part-time soldiers and as a result the Territorials were used to relieve regulars garrisoning the Empire, allowing regiments such as the Royal Dublin Fusiliers to return to Britain. On 9 October the Devons set sail for India, many leaving the British Isles for the first time. One of them was a local man, Private J. Eastabrook, who described his feelings:

'It is wonderful how one becomes imbued with a patriotic and military spirit here. Portions of regiments which have been in the firing line are encamped about a mile from us, and their statements respecting the fighting, and the damnable methods of the Germans, makes one's blood boil, and undoubtedly form a stimulus to the men at home, and make them more determined than ever to prevent at all costs the possibility of such things being allowed to happen here in England...We see and hear a lot more of these things than you do, and hearing matters in their true perspective, appreciate them better. Lord Kitchener has prepared for a long war, and I think he is quite right to do so.'

As the high command shuffled regiments around the world, the BEF was being shuttled across the Channel. In command was Sir John French, a veteran of numerous colonial wars, and directly underneath him were Sir Douglas Haig commanding I Corps and Sir James Grierson commanding II Corps. Grierson died unexpectedly on 17 August and French wished to replace him with Plumer but Kitchener overruled him appointing Sir Horace Smith-Dorrien instead. Under their command were dozens of Torquinians including a substantial number in the 1st Devons which crossed the Channel on 21 August.

Once the BEF arrived it quickly took up position on the far left of the French armies and advanced into Belgium to meet the oncoming Germans. As the Germans marched forward they ran into the BEF at Mons on 23 August in the British Army's first major action. Outnumbered three to one, the highly experienced British soldiers put up a valiant defence, inflicting more casualties than they suffered. German soldiers were mown down in such numbers by the highly accurate British rifle fire that they thought they were facing machine guns. However the BEF was battling against the inevitable and by early afternoon it was forced off the Mons Canal and had to retreat south, where it attempted to fortify its position. Driver A.E. Taylor, of Babbacombe, saw the battle from a distance behind Mons as part of the artillery:

'When we came within sight of Mons the town was being shelled by the Germans, and a part was on fire...We opened fire at 3,000 yards on the German infantry and cavalry, and by what a German officer told our men, we mowed them down like wheat in a field.'

This new defensive position only lasted for hours as the French Fifth Army under General Lanrezac began to retreat leaving the British right flank dangerously exposed. Reluctantly French gave the order to withdraw once more and the BEF began falling back to a stronger position on the Valenciennes to Maubeuge road. Taylor was involved early in the morning of 24 August as the retreat began:

'We went into action in the same position at 3.30 on Monday morning. As soon as our battery opened fire the Germans started shelling. The first two rounds dropped to the rear of our teams, and the third dropped right in the centre of our horses. I was the first driver to be hit. Eight more were wounded soon after...shells were bursting and the bullets dropping as thick as hailstones, our infantry and cavalry suffered heavily, leaving hundreds behind.'

Taylor escaped from Mons along with much of the BEF, however only a number of heroic actions fought over the coming days prevented a larger disaster. The German onslaught continued and the British were forced into a continual retreat. It was a period of immense stress and danger and was only prevented from turning into a wholesale disaster by a number of brave rearguard actions as the BEF retreated out of Belgium and back toward Paris.

At Le Cateau Smith-Dorrien's II Corps fought an action, inflicting heavy losses upon the Germans and saving elements of the BEF from envelopment. At Étreux and Oisny the next day, three companies of the 2nd Battalion Royal Munster Fusiliers held up the Germans for fourteen hours despite being outnumbered six to one. Amongst the chaos, on 28 August near Moÿ-de-l'Aisne, the 12th Lancers charged a dismounted Prussian Dragoons Regiment. A resident of Torquay, Corporal Gilbert Winget, described the scene:

'We followed the Germans for days and gave them no rest when they commenced their retreat, and finally we captured a lot of their transport, and charged their infantry in some open ground, inflicting great loss upon them. Some 300 Germans threw down their arms and surrendered to the regiment, unable to stand against our lances which they dread.'

The cavalry charge described by Winget was one of a number of similar actions fought that autumn, the war still represented previous wars rather than trench warfare. Throughout the following weeks many other actions occurred, each saving elements of the British and French Armies from destruction and costing the Germans precious time in their drive toward Paris.

As the retreating Allied armies desperately attempted to halt the German advance, on the home front recruitment efforts stepped up. Paris was under threat and defeat seemed possible. It was one of the most desperate periods of the war and this was acutely understood. It was during this period that voluntary enlistment peaked, not during the opening days of the war as is commonly believed. Men enlisted in large numbers due to the risk of losing the war rather than because of blind patriotism. The trend in Torquay reflects this; as previously noted Torquay provided a larger proportion of Devon's volunteers than its population would suggest, however its figures were not consistent and large numbers enlisted in two spikes. As in the traditional view, there was a rush to the colours in the first week with sixty-six men enlisting. In the second week figures suffered a large fall as they dropped to just seventeen. This is not surprising as the infrastructure for recruitment was poor and the efforts of the government were still basic and relied on local initiative.

In common with the rest of the country, news of Mons and the Great Retreat spurred recruitment. During the week of the battle, forty-six Torquinians enlisted, followed by forty-eight and fifty-five in the following two weeks. The enlistment boom in Torquay during the Great Retreat never reached the peak of the opening week but in the third week of the boom it was only nine volunteers short and the period showed a higher average than the first three weeks. In the country as a whole recruitment exploded, the week ending 29 August saw over 63,000 enlisting and the following week 174,901, nearly tripling the previous record. Once the threat to Paris ended with victory at the Battle of the Marne, enlistments fell sharply. The week of 9-16 September produced only twenty-five volunteers in Torquay, the following two weeks produced twenty-five between them. The end of the threat to Paris combined with the government tightening requirements to slow down the boom had much to do with this. Weekly figures for the rest of the year are unavailable but from what exists it can be extrapolated that throughout October and November volunteers averaged around thirteen a week. There was a slight increase at the end of November and into December but it was small and numbers remained well below the first two months.

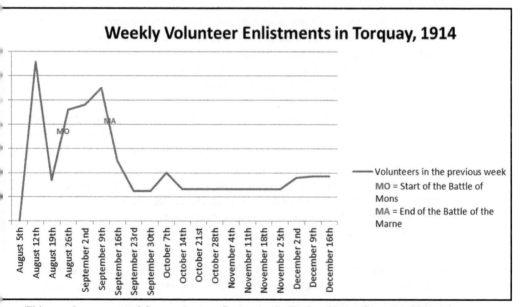

Weekly Volunteer Enlistments in Torquay, 1914

Volunteers in the previous week
MO = Start of the Battle of Mons
MA = End of the Battle of the Marne

This graph was created from volunteer figures in the Torbay News. Care should be taken when looking at the figures for 23 Sept to 16 Dec. These are average enlistment figures based on available data with the exception of 7 October 7 and 2 December which are exact.

Across the country recruitment rates varied massively. Devon, Dorset, Cornwall and Somerset recruited only eleven volunteer battalions amongst them compared to Lancashire alone with thirty-three. Per head of population the regions showed large variances:

Region	Number of Recruits per 10,000 residents
Southern Scotland	237
Midlands Counties	196
Lancashire	178
London and the Home Counties	170
Yorkshire, Durham and Northumberland	150
Ireland (Inc. Ulster, Dublin, Wicklow and Kildare)	127
Torquay	**101**
West of England	88
Southern Ireland (Agricultural Districts)	32

Regional recruitment figures per 10,000 residents until 4 November 1914
Source: Parliamentary Recruiting Committee quoted in Simkins p.112 with Torquay data taken from recruitment data published in the Torbay News throughout 1914.

As previously mentioned Torquay's recruitment figures were substantially larger than its surrounding region and closer to those elsewhere in the country, the prevalence of the leisure industry helping to increase its numbers. Recruitment figures in this industry, which included hotels, amounted to 41.8 per cent of its pre-war workforce by February 1916 contrasting with a national average of 29.4 per cent.

During these crisis days, women came to the fore. A large meeting of women was held at the Pavilion. Doubts about whether the town was contributing enough were expressed and speaking at the meeting was Lady Acland, a well-known local resident:

'We meet at a hour of unexplained anxiety...We are here to ask the women of Torquay to do a very hard thing – to send the men whom they hold dearest to defend their land. Don't let it be said that we in Devon are too soft...to think of the peril through which our country is passing at the moment.'

She continued in an almost Churchillian vein:

'The men are serving in the shops and driving carts. Let us rise and say we will serve in the shops! We will drive the carts! We will see that Torquay doesn't starve! ...Don't let us be seen hanging on the arm of any man who hasn't at least volunteered for the front!'

By all accounts the speech was well received and a number of women stood up and stated how many of their sons had enlisted to widespread applause. The meeting ended with exhortations for the women of Torquay to do everything necessary to ensure their men were doing their duty. The feeling amongst those present was once more that the war was going to be long, hard and bloody.

While the women of Torquay were firing themselves up to do their patriotic duty, sporting life shut down. Torquay Town suspended all play on 31 August and their rivals Babbacombe Town followed suit on 7 September. Torquay Athletic Rugby Club followed suit shortly after in part because fifteen of their players had already enlisted. A hush now fell over the Torquay sporting scene.

On the Western Front the stalwart efforts of the French had blunted the German advance just long enough to give the Allies time to mobilise in force outside Paris. At the Battle of the Marne six French armies and the BEF dealt the Germans a defeat which saved Paris. Corporal Winget wrote of his experiences:

'Under cover of our guns, the regiment got amongst the enemy. The artillery shelled the transport, and the Germans fled. Then we were let loose, and we charged them, bagging 300, one gun, and half a hundred motors and carts. The place was a shambles, the road a mass of huddled animals and men; it was a rout. We had two officers hit, five killed and a few wounded. I broke my lance in half in one man's body. He was wearing a mail shirt I fancy, but my point went straight through…Some Germans were overlooked, hidden beneath corn stooks…so we went round and stuck our lances in every stook; it was fun. We soon cleared them.'

By this point the Germans were in danger of suffering a serious defeat and began a retreat to more defensible positions on the Aisne, marking the end of Germany's best chance to win the war. Here on the Aisne they began to dig trenches. Winget's reports reflect this:

'The 12th was a general action all day, with other brigades joined to ours. It rained very hard, but we scoured the woods and villages and made 1,000 prisoners – men who had been forced to fall out, so rapid had been our advance. A few we killed, but most Germans seemed glad to be taken; they were worn out. On the 13th we took a large village, and from here entered the initial stage of the "Battle of the Rivers". The enemy had succeeded in crossing the Aisne. Here they had strong positions.'

Immediately following their success on the Aisne the Allies attempted to counter-attack with the 1st Devons entering the fray on 14 September. The following day the battalion suffered its first casualties with Captain Luxmoore of Torquay becoming the first officer of the Devons to be wounded; he was hit by shrapnel while attempting to organise his men in their trenches.

As the battle raged, letters began to filter home in increasing numbers. The *Torquay Times* published a letter from Private W. Stone, a former resident of the town and striker for Torquay Town FC. Stone had fought at Mons and had not escaped unscathed:

'I have got one of my fingers blown off but I shall, I hope soon, be fit and to have another cut. I am very sorry to say that my company got terribly cut up at Mons. 72 wounded and 12 killed out of 120 officers and men.'

The losses he describes were not unusual. Despite this he seemed in high spirits:

'I am glad to say that we gave the Germans beans! Their infantry are no good at all. They cannot shoot for toffee! I should be very much pleased to see some of the Torquay boys come out and join us.'

Back in Torquay, Agatha Christie noted:

'Already the casualties had startled and surprised people. A lot of my friends had been soldiers, and had been called up at once. Every day, it seemed, one read in the newspaper that somebody one knew had been killed.'

These visceral effects of war and the so-called 'Rape of Belgium' further hardened attitudes towards Germany. The *Torquay Times* published a letter signed from an 'Englishman' stating:

'Englishmen are asking why Germans and Austrians should be employed in Torquay...They are keeping Englishmen out of work...I should like to know where the patriotism of their English employers comes in. It is very well to say that these foreigners are naturalised Englishmen but blood is thicker than water and I maintain that it is against human nature for a German or an Austrian to have any sympathy with our arms in this war.'

On 11 September a meeting of waiters was held to form an association designed to 'aid employment for waiters at present unemployed and especially to replace German waiters'. The national press supported these ideas with letters printed in *The Times* and *Daily Mail* calling for all German waiters in the country to be sacked. What the German Waiters Association, accused of being a front for spies back in August, had to say about these events we don't know.

Rumours were also appearing in greater numbers of the supposed atrocities perpetrated by German soldiers. A letter from an officer in the BEF to a resident of Paignton was published stating that he'd seen several young girls in a Paris hospital who'd had their hands chopped off by German soldiers. The veracity of these letters should be questioned, many were based upon second hand accounts, but they further worsened the town's opinion and although some reports were fabrications German atrocities were occurring and as a result lent authority to the false reports.

A sensational letter was also published in the *News* from Miss Madeline Lyons, a former resident of Warbro Road, who had been in Mons as governess to Count and Countess de la Roche. They had fled to Torquay when the Germans advanced and after describing their flight, Miss Lyons ended her story with a call for English men to go to Belgium. She recalled:

'The Belgians were expecting the English any moment, as they thought the English would help them. When they left Belgium they had not heard of the arrival of the English. Nobody knew where they were, as it was to be kept a secret from the Belgians. Somebody thought they were at Bevelot, but they did not know. All they knew was that they had crossed the water. The people were very confident that England would help them; in fact they felt they were safer with England than with France.'

Asked if she knew anything about the supposed atrocities:

'It is dreadful but it is true. Some won't believe it, but it is perfectly true. They dragged the women from their homes, which they then set on fire, dragged them miles along the roads, and then hanged them. It was said that they are doing that because they are starving like dogs; they have nothing to eat, and are perfectly brutal.

In contrast to these reports, a German lady in Krefeld wrote to a friend in Torquay, denying the atrocities:

'Germany has been forced to take up arms. The war was prepared a long time ago by your government, France and Russia…As for Belgium, I can tell you that it does not exist anymore. The government is led by German people. I am sure you heard about the ruin of Louvain. You can imagine that the whole civilisation, and last, not least, Germany regrets the loss of precious artistic buildings. But we were forced to do so in self-defence. When our soldiers had taken possession of the town, the white banner was hissed. Our soldiers entered the town, as suddenly private people fired from the houses in all directions. It must have been a dreadful scene. I spoke to some of the wounded compatriots from Louvain who had experienced it.

'Therefore, to prevent that another time, our commanders had to take these apparently severe steps. I will add that the old celebrated town hall was saved by us. The rumours about German cruelties against their enemies are invented. I am nursing in one of the military hospitals. There are Englishmen here. They feel quite comfortable and get just the same eating and nursing as our own people, though they have not deserved it.'

This denial was highly unlikely to have been believed and the general anger boiled over into violence when Albert Spagna, an Italian fruit merchant, visited the Railway Inn in Torre. While there he ended up in an altercation with John Heywood who shouted at him, 'Von German', before Spagna replied, 'Don't call me a German'. Heywood had been drinking heavily and already been thrown out twice when he proceeded to square up to Spagna before taking him outside. What happened next is disputed, reports suggesting the Italian either hit Heywood or Heywood, heavily drunk, fell and injured himself. He was sent to Torbay Hospital with Spagna paying for his fare and later died. The Italian was arrested and found guilty of manslaughter despite the fact that the deceased had no bruises on his body consistent with being hit. Anti-German sentiment in the town had claimed two victims, one dead and one sent to prison for a crime he may not have committed.

With drunks throwing around 'German' as an insult, an unnamed young German lady living in Torquay must have felt relieved to receive a letter from her father in Berlin before being surprised at his strange comments, he wrote:

'We are thankful that our country has been spared from seeing the war…London must be awful. Half of it burned down and the Zeppelins always hovering over the place. Two years ago we spent such a pleasant time in that beautiful city and now it is almost destroyed.'

Ignoring the fact that London was still very much standing, the unnamed Herr continued:

'We are told that Plymouth has also been destroyed by fire. I believe you are near Plymouth. I pray that you're safe.'

Despite his totally inaccurate facts, those about London even being published in *The Times* and described as 'curious', this father's words to his daughter must have given her some support while Torquay continued to become more anti-German by the month. In Germany, a Torquinian living in Bremen, mirroring the experience of living in a hostile environment, seemed to be having a better time. She wrote of the strange feeling of the first months and how it was beginning to change:

'It is all very quiet here, so quiet that we can hardly believe there is war. Now the first wounded are arriving. They tell us the horrors of war. It is awful to hear. I am much worried about you, that perhaps you suffer want. Are prices much higher with you? Yesterday I saw for the first time some English papers. I cannot help thinking of those awful airships and the agony they produce.'

The war was now well into its third month and a movement began to help the Belgians. The town council offered hospitality to any who could make the journey and fundraising efforts gathered pace; women and children in Chelston produced over 200 garments for the people of Belgium and on 17 October the first Belgians arrived, fifty wounded officers on their way to Torbay Hospital with another seventy arriving four days later. All but two attended a concert at the Pavilion where the Belgian national anthem was played and the Belgians joined in a cheer of *'Vive L'Angleterre'* to which George Bernard Shaw, who was sitting in the gallery replied *'Vive Belgique!'* to much amusement.

This period began a fascination for everything Belgian and on 4 November the Pavilion held a cinematographic lecture about 'Brave Little Belgium'. It also had a profound effect on the mind of the young Agatha Christie, leading to her creation of Hercule Poirot. She had thought to herself: 'Why not make my detective a Belgian? There were all types of refugees. How about a refugee police officer?'

In addition to the Belgians, British soldiers flooded into the town. On 1 October ten officers arrived at Stoodley Knowle, owned by Colonel Burn. He had placed the house at the disposal of the Red Cross and it had been requisitioned as a hospital for officers. This first batch of wounded men were joined by a further eight officers and forty other wounded of various ranks on 21 October. Stoodley Knowle was later joined by hospitals at the Mount (later moved to Rockwood), the Manor House, Lyncourt and finally the Western Hospital for Consumptives, all of which were used for officers while the Town Hall was used for rank and file.

Agatha Christie served in the town hall as a nurse during the early months before transferring to a dispensary and it was during these days spent working amongst chemicals and drugs that she began to learn about the poisons that play a prominent role in her writing. Already used to playing host to the sick and infirm, Torquay was quick to adapt to the flood of wounded troops although the effects of modern war were shocking to some. Christie spoke of her early days in the makeshift hospitals:

'The flight of the more elderly would-be nurses was accelerated by the fact that our early cases came in straight from the trenches with field dressings on, and their heads full of lice. Most of the ladies of Torquay had never seen a louse – I had never seen one myself – and the shock of finding these dreadful vermin was far too much for the older dears. The young and tough, however, took it in their stride.'

In addition to the wounded, 400 men of the 43rd (Wessex) Infantry Division arrived en route to India, their presence leading to a minor controversy in true Torquay fashion when, following a 'mothers' meeting' in St Marychurch, the Reverend F.H. Bickersteth Ottley of Saint Matthias drafted a circular warning local ladies of the problems of having soldiers in town. It stated:

> 'We urge you to impress upon your daughters and upon your servants, the great need of a very high standard of Christian modesty and conduct in demeanour and dress at this time of national sorrow, and we would suggest that you should keep your servants and daughters within their homes after sunset.'

For respectable residents of a town like Torquay soldiers could only bring trouble according to the Reverend. Agatha Christie recalled her grandmother worrying, telling her that it was 'So dangerous, dear, walking home by yourself. Anything might happen.' Unfair as such comments were to the professional soldiers of the BEF, they were especially unfair when applied to the part time Territorials, most of whom lived in the south-west and held respectable jobs. It didn't take long for complaints to be heard, with the *Torquay Times* claiming the circular was 'a personal insult to a body of men who…have proved themselves to have all the honourable instincts which British soldiers should have'. Within days the vicar made a hasty apology and the warm welcome continued.

The *laissez faire* nature of the early months was now giving way and talk about potential winter boom seasons was being replaced with stories about the violence of the war. Corporal L.W. Dyer wrote home:

> 'I tell you it has made my heart bleed more than once. Fancy, seeing pieces of men's bodies lying around in all directions, and other poor fellows groaning all around you. People used to say that the South African war was dreadful, but I can assure you that it was child's play compared to this.'

Another letter published on the same day from Private Hopkins of the 1st Devons, featured remarkably similar sentiments:

> 'The war in South Africa was only child's play compared to this. This is war to the death...I don't mind being wounded for old England's sake and if I were alright I would have another go at the German dogs. They can't bear the English bulldogs!'

The *Torquay Times'* editorial reflected:

> 'Torquay is being gradually brought into closer touch with the war, not only geographically but in a social sense. The immensity of this almost worldwide struggle now in progress has perhaps been less realised in this borough than in any other town of the size…Torquay has witnessed little or nothing of the actual preparation for war or the results which have followed the hostilities. Now however things have changed…There are now wounded British soldiers in our midst...The tramp of soldiers' feet and the clatter of the hoofs of war horses are heard in the streets and the sound of the bugle arouses the inhabitants in neighbourhoods in which those who are training for their country's service are quartered.'

On the Western Front, the 1st Devons had spent ten days on the Aisne and were finally withdrawn on 26 September having suffered nearly 100 casualties. With the failure of the Allied counter-offensive, a deadlock developed from the Aisne to Switzerland as primitive trench works were established. Both sides attempted a number of flanking manoeuvres to the north forcing the epicentre of the war steadily towards the Channel while reinforcements flooded into France. Keen to keep the BEF together as one force, Field Marshal French agitated for permission to relocate further north, the geography around the Channel Ports and Flanders was still free of trench works and represented the last opportunity to make a breakthrough. Along with their allies the BEF developed a new plan, to drive into Belgium and turn the German flank. French was granted permission and on 27 September the Devons left the Aisne and headed north to Flanders. While the BEF moved northwards a new problem was causing headaches at sea.

With the outbreak of war Britain and her allies had taken advantage of their naval superiority to conquer the majority of the German colonial empire. Vice-Admiral Maximilian von Spee had been in command of the German East Asia Squadron at Tsingtao before the war but, realising the vulnerability of his base, had refused to return upon the declaration of war; instead he despatched the light cruiser *Emden* into the Indian Ocean to prey upon Allied shipping and took the majority of his force into the Pacific. After an aborted attack on New Zealanders operating around German Samoa, Von Spee resolved to cross the Pacific in an attempt to return to Germany via South America rather than risk British controlled waters. His squadron arrived off the coast of Chile in early October and soon began preying upon Allied shipping.

Learning of his location the Admiralty ordered Rear-Admiral Sir Christopher Craddock's South Atlantic Squadron to intercept him. Craddock split his squadron in two and sailed through the Straights of Magellan to locate his opponent. Under his command were the armoured cruisers *Good Hope* and *Monmouth*, his only modern ship the light cruiser *Glasgow* and a converted passenger liner the *Otranto*. Craddock's squadron was outdated, aside from the *Glasgow*, outgunned and crewed by naval reservists. In comparison Von Spee's squadron was modern, heavily armed and crewed by professionals. On 1 November the two forces blundered into each other off the Chilean town of Coronel. The battle was a total disaster for the Royal Navy, the *Good Hope* and *Monmouth* were sunk and in exchange for 1,570 dead the British squadron wounded just three German sailors as the outgunned and inferior British force was scattered.

It was also the bloodiest day of the war so far for Torquay, eleven Torquinians went down with their ships. On board the *Good Hope* two Torquinians died while on the *Monmouth* nine were lost. For a proud naval town such as Torquay this was a painful loss. In the colonial wars of the nineteenth century the town would have been unlucky to lose eleven men in an entire war and Torquay's single day losses at Coronel would not be surpassed for nearly two years.

On the Western Front Erich von Falkenhayn had now taken command of the German Armies and immediately recognised the opportunity that Flanders represented, launching an offensive to capture the Channel ports before running into the BEF at the small Belgian town of Ypres in the First Battle of Ypres.

The BEF was in a bad state, the huge expenditure of artillery shells that modern warfare required had depleted its supplies and for much of the battle the BEF was heavily outgunned and forced to hide behind any shelter its soldiers could find or in makeshift waterlogged trenches. From these defences they once again relied upon their superior rifle fire as they held on by their fingertips.

Arriving in Flanders the 1st Devons were assigned to Givenchy, to the south of Ypres. The Germans shelled their positions and communication to the rear was immensely difficult. Frequent assaults were launched and on 23 October a 'perfect tornado of shells' descended upon Givenchy and while the French to the south were driven from their trenches, the Devons held firm. When the French pushed up new forces to reoccupy their trenches they found the Devons covered in gunpowder and mud but still holding their position. The heaviest fighting yet occurred on 25 October with artillery raining down upon the British soldiers defending with little more than their rifles. Again the French wavered and gave ground but the Devons stood firm and by the following evening the fighting around Givenchy began to wear down. The Devons had suffered nearly 250 casualties and, of the officers who had landed in August, only a dozen were still in active service. The first experience of a major battle for the Torquinians serving in the Devons had been a bloody one.

Fighting carried on around Ypres until the beginning of November and the Devons were continually in action, losing another hundred casualties as the BEF clung on to their Belgian toehold. By now they had been joined by their comrades in the 2nd Devons who arrived from Cairo. Having recently been deployed in Egypt, the battalion found the winter weather harsh and large numbers began suffering from frostbite.

On 18 November Corporal Winget, Torquay's most vivid chronicler of 1914, fell in battle. While desperately defending against a German assault, shrapnel had ripped into Winget's side, badly wounding him and piercing one of his lungs. As Winget lay dying so did the best of the BEF, its blood draining into the waterlogged Flanders fields. What had been the best-trained army in the world was slowly bleeding to death in the carnage surrounding Ypres.

When First Ypres finally ground to a halt the 'Old Contemptibles' almost ceased to exist having suffered roughly 58,000 casualties in addition to those already lost. A large majority of those who had served before the war were now either dead or invalided. However the desperate fighting around Ypres had foiled the attempt to capture the Channel ports and this small town's name would soon come to be intimately linked with the entire British war effort.

When Falkenhayn ended his operation the BEF was at breaking point, had he persisted there was every chance the Germans would have broken through and found the road to Calais open. Douglas Haig who was involved throughout, would remember this missed opportunity which contributed to his prolonging many battles long beyond their usefulness. The German defeat at Ypres marked the end of the war of manoeuvre as the trench systems that had developed throughout the battle began to link up with those already established to the south. Although no one day during the battle matched Torquay's losses at Coronel, Corporal Winget and his comrades would be the first of many from the town to give their lives around Ypres.

The battle for Ypres continued to cost lives, while the people of Torquay began to wonder what should be made of Christmas. It seemed wrong to celebrate in the old way but the *Torquay Times* urged 'Christmas as usual' stating:

> 'The coming Christmas may not appropriately be one of great frivolity; it may not be a time to spend money in the giving of unnecessary presents. But that should not imply that we should stifle the feelings of goodwill.'

In early December it was announced that men of the Argyll and Sutherland Highlanders and the Highland Light Infantry were due to arrive in the town but this order was rescinded and instead the 1st Royal Dublin Fusiliers arrived from India. Lieutenant Colonel Rooth, commander of the battalion, ordered his men to 'prove that, despite their reputation to the contrary, Irishmen were capable of living well, as well as fighting well'. He needn't have worried as the Fusiliers soon made many friends. With their arrival Torquay took on the feel of a garrison town, full to the brim with troops billeted in lodging houses alongside dozens of wounded soldiers in the war hospitals.

A few days later Vice-Admiral von Spee finally met his end off the Falkland Islands. He had arrived to raid the settlement of Stanley unaware that British forces were present. Unlike the outdated and inexperienced British forces at Coronel, the British squadron he met was experienced and outgunned their opponents. As the British ships entered battle, on board the *Cornwall* a young Torquinian by the name of Townsend got his first experience of war:

> 'The *Glasgow* first opened fire on the smaller German ships, then the *Kent*, and a moment later the *Cornwall*, with her foremost guns. Later we went into independent firing. The ship we were engaging was the *Leipzig*, the *Kent* went in pursuit of the *Nürnberg*...At length we shot away the *Leipzig*'s main mast, then her foremost funnel, and later the top of her second funnel. About half way through the engagement she caught fire, and we witnessed several explosions on board. As soon as we ceased firing, after just four hours of it, we lowered and sent away all our boats for survivors, but they only picked up four men.'

The battle was almost an exact reversal of Coronel with ten British sailors killed compared to more than 1,500 at Coronel. Along with the *Leipzig* another three German ships were sunk including von Spee's flagship the *Scharnhorst*, the admiral going down with his ship. Another two German ships were captured and scuttled and two small German ships escaped to be later destroyed. The previous month the *Emden*, which had been operating in the Indian Ocean, was also captured ending a famous career which the *Torquay Times* reflected upon:

> 'Without exception, those who had the misfortune to fall under the power of the Captain of the *Emden*, speak of him as a courteous and honourable gentleman. He played the game, and did not do so as many of his fellow countrymen have done and are doing – disregarding the elementary rules of warfare. Although most individuals and things that bear the name German, are repugnant to us just now, there will be in the hearts of many a touch of sporting sympathy for Captain Müller.'

No such thoughts were expressed about von Spee. Townsend stated that while loading their guns men had shouted at each other 'Come on lads! Remember the *Good Hope* and the *Monmouth*!'

Despite the destruction of von Spee's squadron, the Kaiser's navy still posed a serious threat in the storm-tossed waters of the North Sea and displayed this in dramatic fashion by raiding the North-East on the morning of 16 December. The raid was designed to lure a detachment of the Royal Navy into a pitched battle with the German High Seas Fleet allowing it to be destroyed piecemeal. The fleet had weighed anchor off Dogger Bank and from there a detachment led by Vice-Admiral Franz von Hipper had sailed towards the coastline, the main fleet hanging back ready to intercept any forces sent south.

At roughly 8am the *Derfflinger* and *Von der Tann* opened fire on Scarborough, indiscriminately shelling prominent buildings including the Grand Hotel. Shells rained down, damaging houses and businesses as civilians fled. After half an hour the raiders departed, leaving behind a burning town and the bodies of the dead and injured. Seventeen people died and ninety-nine were wounded. Scarborough had not been a military town and the shelling of it was illegal, more importantly British civilians had died at the hands of a foreign navy for the first time in 247 years. Shortly afterwards Whitby suffered a similar fate and then Hartlepool. When Hipper sailed away from Hartlepool, 1,150 shells had been fired, 86 civilians had been killed, and 424 wounded, in West Hartlepool alone more than 300 houses had been damaged.

Mr F. Grey, a Torquinian, was holidaying twelve miles away and immediately motored down to see the damage. He was particularly struck by how many children had been killed and also by the number of unexploded shells strewn around the town. The raids shocked Torquay. Scarborough was the northern mirror of Torquay, both having a population of around 40,000, an economy dominated by tourism and possessing an exclusive hotel named the Grand. Being so similar in nature, the raid provoked feelings of anger and fear. Mayor Towell attempted to express this by sending a telegram which read: 'Torquay sincerely sympathises with your inhabitants on your loss of life, injury to your persons, and damage to property, recently caused by Germans' utter disregard of international law.' True feelings ran more passionately against what many believed to be a criminal act.

On the Western Front some soldiers began to think of home and an end to the war. Private S. Mann of the Queen's Westminsters wrote home to his parents in Torquay:

> 'I have at last had my baptism of fire. When we went into the firing trenches it was snowing like fury. The trenches are not as bad as one imagines; the only trouble is the German snipers. They come up to within 60 yards and pot you off directly you expose yourself...Are there any rumours of peace at home? Regular soldiers here think that we shall be home by Christmas. I myself do not think it at all possible.'

Mann's letter home is not evidence of the 'over by Christmas' theory of the war, the regulars he was fighting alongside were used to short colonial wars and their thoughts may well have been wishful thinking more than anything else. Mann's view that peace was off the agenda was much closer to mainstream thought. Another letter sent home was from Ernest Beer, serving with the Royal Army Medical Corps:

'As may be expected, we are not having everything our way. The stench all along our line of march from the dead horses was unbearable, and the sad sights of women, both aged and young, with little children, fleeing from their houses, is enough to stir the hardest of hearts. The Germans have committed the most brutal and barbarous acts imaginable. They have destroyed homes, and the women have been outraged unsparingly, and the husbands of these women who are not at the front are ruthlessly murdered if they protest. Unless people see these things one would hardly credit that such acts would be perpetrated by a so-called civilised race…I have only seen one Torquay chap in my travels, but my chum is a lad from Newton Abbot. Well, I am quite satisfied with my experiences, but I think this will appease my appetite for adventure…Let us hope this horrible affair will soon be over for the benefit of all concerned.'

In another letter sent home over the festive period, Private A.P. Jones was very clear about the brutality of the war:

'We know what real war is by this time – you can hardly call it war, for it is more like a hell of fire...I am in the advance clearing hospital and we all take our turn in going to the trenches for the wounded. Some of the men who are brought in have wounds too gruesome to mention…You would not recognise the soldiers if you could only see them come out of the trenches, for most of them are covered from head to toe with mud…Sometimes the wounded lie in the trenches for hours at a time, for the firing is so persistent that one cannot possibly reach them.'

The fact that these letters were being openly published shows that although some information was censored, the public was far from being shielded from the grim reality of the war. When Christmas finally arrived there was a sober atmosphere although the presence of the Dublins was enjoyed by many, their Irish craic and exotic stories of India providing much entertainment.

On the Western Front, Torquinians made do as best as they could. Private J. Redmore of the 2nd Devons, wrote home:

'It is raining nearly every day, or else it is freezing cold. Christmas Day it was freezing, and it looked rather good to look upon it in the morning, something like an old Christmas. It was our turn in the trenches on Christmas Day, so we kept it up on the 23rd, and we had rather a decent time, under the circumstances. Our regiment made a good name for themselves when they were in the trenches last time, carrying out an attack on the Germans, and finishing up with a bayonet charge, driving the Germans out of their trenches like a lot of rabbits.'

By the time the BEF ended its operations for the year it had suffered 89,969 casualties, more than in the Crimean War, Indian Mutiny and the Second Boer War combined. Despite this it was steadily growing in size, regular battalions had returned from the Empire and the vanguard of the Canadian Expeditionary Force – 32,000 strong and the largest army to have ever crossed the Atlantic – had arrived. The increased size of the BEF now required it to be split into two armies, Douglas Haig taking command of First Army and Horace Smith-Dorrien, Second Army.

Torquay had changed almost beyond recognition. Its tourist industry was much reduced and the town had taken on the appearance of a garrison. The previously thriving German community had suffered greatly and those who remained felt like strangers in what had previously been their home. The demands of the armed forces had been high and losses for the year were at least thirty-eight men. Many in the town had already lost loved ones or suffered financial damage as a result of the war but none more so than the Belgians. A Belgian soldier recovering in Torquay over Christmas looked back on life since war had broken out:

'Before the war broke out I had a wife and three children – two girls and a boy, aged 10, 7 and $4^{1}/_{2}$ and all I have got now is my life and my trousers. I landed in England like that. My wife and three children were murdered by the Germans. My house was burnt to the ground and every stick I had was gone. But I am going back to get my own back. I don't care what happens to my life, as long as I can get my own back before I am pushed off. It is not fighting I have seen but when I try to go to sleep at night it is like hell, and I cannot. I keep thinking of a few weeks ago, when I was happy with my wife and family, and tonight I am left all alone.'

His story was sadly all too common during the first year of the war and things would get worse before they got better. The scene was now set for escalation.

Chapter 2

1915 - Education

'For five months we have been living a life strangely different from that of former years. Every month has brought the reality of the war nearer to us in all senses. In August the whole thing seemed like a fantastic dream, a piece of sensational fiction. Now it is a terrible overshadowing fact. We are all confident of the final result as we ever were. But by this time we have got so far along the dark way that leads to victory, that we understand the greatness and long endurance by which the victory is to be won.'
New Year letter from Archdeacon Simms of Saint Luke's Church

Britain entered 1915 in a sombre mood, however her fighting spirit persisted and, having thwarted the invasion of France, the Allies now resolved to go on the offensive. In Torquay the Dublins received their orders to depart and in a symbolic act handed over their colours for safekeeping with Mayor Towell claiming that it was 'a great honour that a non-military town should be asked to take charge of the colours of such a famous regiment'. They left by train at 1am on 15 January with a large number of locals staying up to see them off. Many Dubliners were disappointed to be leaving with one soldier reflecting 'It was very kind of the Torquay people to treat us so well, but in some cases it is a cruel kindness. We wish they were all on board the train.' Lieutenant Colonel Rooth said: 'Neither I, nor the officers, the non-commissioned officers, and men of this battalion will ever forget our much too short stay in Torquay.' Little did anyone present that day know how few would return.

Attention now turned elsewhere as the aftermath of the raids on Scarborough, Hartlepool and Whitby threw Torquay into a bout of invasion fear. The *Torbay News* reproduced a ridiculous article from the *Daily Express* warning of a possible German landing in Paignton. Rumours of a German submarine off Berry Head began circulating and a tale about a mysterious 'German' residing on the road to Teignmouth sparked off a round of frenzied accusations. Apparently this German had 'visited various stores, buying small quantities of petrol, which were secretly conveyed to caves, and from which the submarine, much talked about, was supplied'. The rumour even reached as far as the House of Commons.

While ridiculed in the *Torquay Times* the rumour about submarine activity was partly true. At the start of the year HMS *Formidable* had been sunk by *U-24*, off Start Point. In rough seas the Brixham trawler *Provident* under Captain William Piller stumbled across one of *Formidable*'s lifeboats and saved seventy-one men. It was from these men that rumours of U-boat activity began to spread. On another occasion a submarine had been seen lying in wait near Torquay. It was stalking the Glasgow steamer *Strathay*, which was sheltering in the bay while travelling to New York, however the submarine soon disappeared.

Finally on 18 February the German government declared the waters around Britain to be a war zone and that Allied shipping would be sunk without warning. The naval raids, the loss of *Formidable* and the declaration of the war zone spooked Torquay. A lady wrote to the *Torquay Times* demanding to know if invasion plans had been drafted and Lord Fortescue, Lord Lieutenant of Devon, was forced to state:

'He knew no more than the audience about the possibility of a raid from the Channel...He concluded that therefore the military and naval authorities did not think it likely that there would be any attempt at landing or anything of that kind in this part of the country...The enemy would not hesitate to bombard Torquay or Paignton if they thought they could do so without risk to themselves or their ships. The conditions of Torquay and Scarborough are not unalike. Both were well known seaside resorts with great natural attractions, had a certain number of troops in them and just enough in the way of signal stations for the Germans to find an excuse for throwing shells into the town.'

Lying deep within the English Channel, any German attempt to shell or invade Torquay was unlikely so long as the Royal Navy continued to exist but this failed to stop speculation, even the council joined the debate. While more measured than the public, they began to plan for an invasion, notices would be posted around the town warning the inhabitants to keep outside lighting to a minimum; in the case of an attack citizens were advised not to run out into the streets but to take refuge in basements; churches and factories would warn of an attack by sounding their hooter or ringing their bells and any troops in the area, police, VTC, firemen or special constables would then assemble to meet the invading forces.

In addition to sparking invasion fears, Scarborough spurred men into volunteering. Norman Cliff who had earlier been rejected and failed to reapply due to his mother's machinations, suddenly felt the need to volunteer once more:

'Out of the blue, German warships attacked Scarborough and Whitby, and that
settled it. I foresaw a possible similar attack on Torquay, and was convinced that
I must defend my home in the only way that seemed possible.'

In a display of bravado worthy of youth, Cliff rejected the recruitment officer's offer of a cushy administrative job and demanded to see service, resulting in his being enlisted in the Grenadier Guards.

While Torquay was busy worrying about German soldiers marching down the Strand, one of her native sons continued his rise to prominence. The expansion of the BEF had resulted in the creation of V Corps and Herbert Plumer was given command, receiving his first battlefield commission of the war. Assigned to the Second Army, Plumer and V Corps were dispatched to the Ypres Salient where he would remain for much of the rest of the war, becoming almost inseparable from that haunted town. Upon arriving, contrary to the popular stereotype of the generals as uncaring detached figures, Plumer was greatly distressed at the state of his men, writing home: 'The men are having a very bad time! The mud is awful and the state of the trenches indescribable.' He immediately set to work in stamping his authority upon the situation.

Elsewhere Torquay's growing Belgian population saw in the New Year by sending

King Albert a message, to which they received a reply:

> 'The King has received the address, in which you tell him, in the most exquisite terms of delicacy, the sentiments of loyalty in his dear soldiers and dear compatriots staying at Torquay. Deeply touched with such a gracious expression of sympathy, the King thanks you very much.'

They were also honoured by a visit from Count D'Alviella, the Vice-President of the Belgian Senate.

In late January the first trouble relating to the new military presence occurred. Two men of the 7th Devons, Private Harris and Private Pullman were patrolling the corner between Torquay train station and Torbay Road. They were armed with rifles and, reflecting the recent invasion fears, were on the lookout for 'the presence of enemy ships or aircraft and any illicit signalling'. Their orders were to apprehend a special car that was supposed to be going through the area.

That evening a motorcar containing Lieutenant Arthur Hart of the Royal Navy and Lieutenant Ernest Simpson of the Army Service Corps, totally unrelated to the orders, attempted to join Torbay Road before being stopped. An altercation ensued with Pullman exclaiming, 'if you move your car I will shoot.' The argument continued and Pullman believed that the men in the motorcar had moved their rifles to be 'at the ready'. As the stand-off continued a crowd began to gather as Hart angrily exclaimed: 'Can't you see that I'm a British naval officer? I have letters to prove who I am!' before Harris replied rudely: 'I don't want to see any letters. Stand there until my colour sergeant comes and shut your yap!' Hart angrily snapped back about being the man's superior officer. At this point a shot was fired. The bullet passed through Hart before striking Simpson, killing Hart instantly with Simpson dying later at Torquay Hospital.

At the inquest, in the absence of any firm evidence that the killing was deliberate, both privates were found innocent and a verdict of accidental death was reached, Harris claiming that the shot was the result of being nudged by someone in the crowd. Following this tragic incident, fears of invasion slowly receded from the public imagination.

The war was affecting more than the British population by now, a young German named Herr Bellardi who had spent the previous few years in Torquay was killed in February. Bellardi had been serving on board the SMS *Blücher* when it was sunk by HMS *Lion* and his parents wrote to the family he had been staying with for news about their son. In a sign that some friendships survived the war, the English family found a German prisoner who had witnessed Bellardi's final moments:

> 'Your son bore himself with bravery and courage to the last. As the end of our fine ship approached I found myself with your son midships on the upper deck. The vessel began to list. On the command "All men out of the ship" your son sprang overboard without a lifesaving vest. I remained on board, and saw an enemy's shell strike where your son must have been. After the smoke and the column of water had been cleared off I could not see anyone in the water. Then I jumped overboard. Before your son left the ship he gave me his hand saying "who

knows whether we shall see each other again.'"

Bellardi is the only verified German casualty that Torquay suffered during the war but his death was just as tragic as any of the British losses.

On 23 April, the rumours about the mysterious 'German' on the road to Teignmouth were finally put to rest when he wrote a humorous letter to the *Torquay Times*:

> 'I had hoped that common sense of the public would have eventually supervened, but for the special information of those persons who still believe (or still wish to believe) that the occupants of this house are German spies or in any way connected with Germany, I would like to state emphatically and clearly that I am *not* a German or a spy. I am a professional musician...The fact that I purchased a Labrador exactly four days before the war broke out does not necessarily brand me a spy, and I should like to assure the Torquay public that it is quite safe to visit the place. They will not be shot or blown up...No police have been assassinated, and so far as an officer and eight men of the East Lancashire Regiment have been able to ascertain, there has been no signalling.'

During this period, a number of famous figures descended upon the town, Sir Arthur Conan Doyle gave a speech about 'The Great Battles of the War', Hilare Belloc gave lectures on 6 May and William Le Queux, whose novels had done much to provoke the invasion fear, also gave speeches on the supposed spy peril. The presence of such nationally famous figures in Torquay may seem unusual but such was the standing of the town that these visits were nothing unusual.

Back on the Western Front on 10 March the BEF entered its first major engagement of the year at Neuve Chapelle. Now in command of First Army, it was Douglas Haig's first opportunity to put his ideas into practice. Haig was a traditional officer determined to force a decisive battle that would return the war to its previous mobility. Alongside this emphasis on a decisive offensive came a view of warfare that initially de-emphasised the role of technology and firepower. During the early years of the war Haig and his fellow officers would make many mistakes following these ideas, however they were facing the unprecedented challenge of adapting to the requirements of modern warfare while lacking much of the equipment and experience to fight it.

The development of the BEF from the small-scale professional force of 1914 to the highly trained conscript army that defeated Germany is best explained through the 'learning curve' theory. This suggests that throughout the war the BEF was ascending a learning curve, constantly learning from mistakes and developing new tactics and technologies that would ultimately peak in 1918. At the same time its commanders were learning from their mistakes and becoming more proficient at combining these factors into a war-winning strategy. Although not a smooth ascent, indeed it is better seen as a generally upward trend with peaks and troughs, the learning curve is a useful theory to employ against popular assumptions of 'lions led by donkeys'. As the first offensive since the onset of trench warfare, Neuve Chapelle marks the beginning of the BEF's ascent up the learning curve.

Originally planned as a minor operation to relieve the French, Haig expanded its aims 'so as to include objectives whose capture, it might seem, would have far-reaching consequences', but artillery and shell shortages ensured the battle would still be concentrated on a relatively narrow front. A number of innovations were present, including aircraft bombing in support of the infantry, distribution of maps marking objectives and the first use of a lifting artillery barrage; where artillery fire was concentrated on one position before leaping forward to a secondary position allowing the infantry to follow.

The 2nd Devons were amongst the battalions that entered the fray that morning. The battle opened at 7.30am with a hurricane artillery bombardment, a chronic lack of shells ruling out prolonged firing. At 8.50am the barrage switched to the second line of defences and the 2nd Middlesex and 2nd Scottish Rifles went over the top, followed by the Devons ten minutes later. To the south a hole nearly a mile wide was ripped open in the German defences as the artillery tore into the barbed wire and the British infantry were upon the Germans before they could react. In the Devons' sector much of the wire had barely been touched and the 2nd Middlesex, clambering through it, met a hailstorm of machine-gun fire taking heavy casualties, as did the left flank of the 2nd Scottish Rifles. Fortunately the right wing of the Scots found an area where the wire was broken and poured in, the Devons following and giving no mercy. They soon broke through the trenches and were fighting their way eastwards towards Neuve Chapelle.

It was now 11am and Neuve Chapelle was already in British hands with the Devons advancing towards the village. By 1pm they had advanced past it but communications to headquarters had been cut and the artillery barrage had failed to lift forward. The opportunity for further advance was lost and the Devons were ordered to dig in. Problems also emerged to the rear as the corps commanders overly micromanaged the battle, the lack of communications causing immense problems with managing large formations of men. It was early afternoon before orders were given to continue the assault, by which point the Germans had recovered from their initial shock. Inevitably the rest of the afternoon and the following day saw little progress and the battle soon ground to a halt.

For a gain just three miles long and one mile deep, 12,000 British soldiers became casualties. The Devons lost 9 officers and 247 soldiers, amongst them four Torquinians, but had performed admirably. After the battle they were greeted with questions of 'What regiment?' on the reply of 'Devons' came shouts of 'Good old Devons! Well done Devons!'. Ironically the shell shortage had contributed greatly to the initial breakthrough. The short, heavy bombardment left the defenders unable to react to the advancing infantry, allowing those soldiers advancing where the barbed wire had been cut to quickly capture the German trenches. Although it was not immediately recognised, when applied properly these 'hurricane' bombardments would form a critical part of the BEF's ascent up the learning curve.

A month later the Germans launched the Second Battle of Ypres, their only large-scale attack on the BEF of 1915. On 22 April with the wind blowing favourably, the Germans opened the battle by deploying a new secret weapon: poison gas. Its effect was immediate. Two French divisions fled in panic and only the stout defence of the Canadians prevented a major breakthrough. Throughout the night British and German forces traded positions back and forth in a bloody melee. Plumer's V Corps was in the thick of the fighting but he had only limited control and the majority of decisions were taken by commanders on the front lines. The battle continued throughout the following day and into a third as the Germans flooded the defenders with even greater clouds of poison gas and a huge artillery bombardment.

Plumer had now gained a stronger hold over the battle and, alongside his superior, Smith-Dorrien, believed that if battle continued with such ferocity they must retreat to the gates of Ypres itself and hold the line there. Throughout the battle Sir John French sent confusing orders, switching between counter-attacking and following his subordinates' suggestions. Becoming frustrated, Smith-Dorrien penned a letter suggesting that unless French could produce more troops then a retreat must be organised. French's relationship with Smith-Dorrien collapsed and he ordered him to hand over control of the battle to Plumer. Although far from happy with French's conduct, Plumer took command and continued to advocate pulling back to Ypres. French finally authorised the withdrawal and throughout 1-3 May Plumer pulled his soldiers back.

Three days later Smith-Dorrien was ordered to hand over control of Second Army to Plumer. Torquay now possessed one of the three most influential men in the BEF, with only French outranking Plumer, and Haig nominally his equal.

Fighting continued in front of Ypres until 25 May when a final attack was beaten off and the Germans wound down their effort. Throughout these desperate battles a further nine Torquinians had fallen. During the retreat Plumer had apparently noticed a three-year-old child playing on the battlefield with German shells falling nearby. He sent an orderly to get the child and when it was brought to him the child was friendly and began to pat him on his face. Plumer laughed and took the child back to headquarters where it was later discovered to have strayed from the parents who were working in a neighbouring field despite the danger. Whether this story was true is debatable, however it made for an excellent propaganda piece.

Ypres had been held once more but the noose had tightened, the BEF's defences were now at its gates with German artillery overlooking the town from all the high ground surrounding it. The political importance of retaining this last corner of Belgium was immense and Plumer set to work on improving the defences and carefully planning a number of diversionary attacks. These included the laying of telephone and telegraph lines in triplicate, leaping barrages of artillery and detonating mines under the German positions; wireless communications and steel helmets were also used for the first time in Second Army. These experiments, although only small in scale, were soon spreading throughout the BEF. Small improvements such as these was further evidence of the army moving along the learning curve. With Second Army strengthening its hold on the shattered city, Plumer began to settle into his role as one of the senior commanders on the Western Front.

On the opposite side of Europe, the navy had been heavily engaged in the Dardanelles since the middle of March with the aim of capturing Constantinople. After two weeks of limited bombardment, an Anglo-French fleet had steamed up the straits to clear the way of mines and artillery. The advance soon turned into a disaster. Poor reconnaissance resulted in the fleet being unaware of new minefields that had been laid and their minesweepers failed to clear them. As a result a number of British and French warships were lost as they hit mines in the narrow straits and were shelled from Turkish forts on both coastlines. The naval attempt to force the straits was abandoned and instead it was decided that the army was to land and clear the region of Turkish forts allowing the minefields to be swept free of enemy fire. The place where the soldiers were to land was named Gallipoli.

A Torquinian, A.B. Dale was serving with the Australians and had recently arrived in Egypt 600 miles to the south. Dale had little love for the country he was garrisoned in:

'The customs of the natives are the study of a lifetime and once seen are never forgotten. Their ways are disgusting, degrading and filthy. They are born thieves, and are brought up from babyhood to consider thieving their mode of living. They are cunning, scheming, resourceful, persistent and insistent. They will ask prices ten times higher than is reasonable and custom expects one to beat them down, disputing and bargaining until one is tired.'

Still not everything was bad in Egypt:

'The Devons are out here, and I have met a good many Torquay boys who are strangers to me. There is much of interest to be seen. The Pyramids are marvellous...You see many strange sights, and have good rides on the camels.'

In the coming weeks Dale might well have looked back upon Egypt and wished he was still there because the Australians were about to embark for the chaos at Gallipoli, where dreams of Constantinople would fade and nations would be forged.

The main assault came from British and French forces landing on the tip of the Gallipoli Peninsula at Cape Helles. Further north the Australia and New Zealand Corps (ANZACs) would land and attempt to cut off the Turkish troops from their line of retreat. The majority of the British forces present were Territorial or ANZAC but amongst the few regulars present was Torquay's honorary battalion, the 1st Royal Dublin Fusiliers, which was involved in the initial landings. Travelling towards the coastline in open-topped boats, the Dublins suffered horrific casualties as machine-gun positions on the cliffs overlooking the beach opened fire. Most men failed to get out of their landing boats and many that did fell into deep water and drowned. Lieutenant Colonel Rooth was killed during the landing and the battalion suffered 600 casualties in the first two days including nearly all their officers. Private Fox of the Dublins writing to a friend in Torquay described the scene:

'The Turks were waiting for us. We had to land under heavy rifle fire. They mowed our regiment down in dozens. The greatest loss was our leaders. They left us only about three officers. It was an appalling sight. I was wounded in the trenches. It is pretty hot out here – not such a picnic as we thought.'

Lance Sergeant A. Morrison also wrote to a Torquinian:

'By God we did not half go through it in landing. It was like going through Hell itself to get ashore, and half the regiment were "knocked out" before we reached land. I got ashore all right and when attacking some of the Turkish trenches was wounded in the right thigh, but am going along all right, and expect to be back at the front in about a month's time. Lieutenant Colonel Rooth and nearly all our officers were killed, and I think it will be all fresh faces when we come back for our colours after this job is finished. We were fighting for forty-eight hours without a stop after we landed and we used the bayonet every chance we got.'

Only 40 out of the 1,100 men who stayed in Torquay would return to claim their colours. At the end of that day none of the initial objectives had been taken and the British and French remained huddled on the beaches where they landed. After a brief respite the First Battle of Krithia was launched on 28 April; another miserable failure, it ended the chance for a quick breakout. When the news of the Dublins' casualties was announced in Torquay it was greeted with much sorrow, the regiment having been referred to throughout the year as 'Our Dublins'. The battalion's regimental flags were draped with black crepe and Mayor Towell sent letters of condolence to the regimental headquarters.

On the evening of 12 May things went from bad to worse. The battleship *Goliath*, anchored off Cape Helles, was sunk by the Turkish destroyer *Muavenet-i Milliye*, with at least eight Torquinians being killed, the most casualties since Coronel. What had been designed as a quick operation to knock Turkey out of the war was becoming as bogged down as the Western Front. Battles were fought throughout the spring and summer and soldiers would linger on the beaches until the end of the year but any opportunity to defeat Turkey had been lost. The sacrifices made by the Australians and New Zealanders at Gallipoli would soon form the basis of a growing national identity in those countries.

As the Gallipoli campaign ground on the BEF was engaged in a number of small-scale operations. On 9 May it fought the battle of Aubers Ridge followed by the Battle of Festubert. Results were less than satisfactory and to excuse this failure, French leaked information that the BEF was critically short of shells resulting in *The Times* openly criticising the government. A week later the *Daily Mail* also attacked Kitchener. This public criticism became known as the 'Shells Crisis' and would play a significant role in coming political turmoil. Shortly after Festubert, Private Richards wrote to the *Torquay Times* describing how, out of four friends who had enlisted at the start of the war, only he now survived:

'You know Fred, Charlie Walker, Harry Hudson and I joined up from Torquay the same day. We have always been together, sharing each other's blankets and food, and always marched in the same section. We lost Harry at Neuve Chapelle. Since then Charlie, Fred and I have been chums. On the 9th of May we had orders to advance about 700 yards across open country amid a perfect hail of bullets and machine-gun fire. We all got over safely and were together all the day. That night we had to line the parapet several times to repulse the enemy. At 5.30 on the 10th we had orders to line the parapet again. Fred and Charlie stood side by side. Charlie was killed instantly, being shot through the head. He had hardly fallen when poor Fred fell across him, also shot through the head. Neither spoke and death was instantaneous – so two chums died at the same moment...You can realise my own feelings when I say I have lost all here now.'

Harry, Charlie and Fred were just three of the thousands of casualties suffered throughout the year but their sacrifice reveals how even before the more publicised sacrifice of the Pals Battalions whole groups of friends were dying alongside each other in the trenches.

Shortly thereafter the last Liberal government in Britain's history fell as Asquith's government, struggling under questions over its conduct of the war, was replaced by a Liberal-Conservative coalition headed by Asquith. The Torquay establishment was critical of the media's role and Councillor Smeardon suggested:

> 'The Library Committee ought to consider the advisability of excluding the *Daily Mail* and *The Times* from the Public Library, at least until the end of the war. Such a protest would evidence the opinion of the Council of the manner in which Lord Kitchener had been attacked. Considering what he had done for the army and the nation during the last nine or ten months, the attack of the *Daily Mail* was despicable.'

The rest of the council adopted the proposal with only one objection and the decision was taken to send a letter of appreciation to Lord Kitchener.

Since the previous year volunteer numbers had been steadily declining and a debate over conscription began to emerge. One local writing under the pen name of 'Patriot' demanded its introduction, showing that support was growing, however a second letter by Eddie Mallet, showed that it was still far from accepted by the majority:

> 'Sir, "Patriot" is no more disgusted with shop serving and theatre building shirkers than are many others, including myself; but his suggested remedy, conscription, would in my opinion prove a greater curse than leaving the "slacker" to his fate. Without conscription there would have been no Kaiserism; and to set up the very monster which we have pledged our existence to crush would be to put a date to the day of our decline. England's greatness has been raised upon the liberty, of the subject – even to the liberty of serving one's country, or not.'

As the conscription debate continued, a greater controversy erupted. On 7 May following the German submarine rules of engagement declared earlier in the year, *U-20* sunk the RMS *Lusitania* off the coast of Ireland. When she went down 1,198 passengers died including 128 Americans. There is no evidence that any Torquinians were amongst the number, however Torquay residents, Mr and Mrs Babbage, were due to travel on the *Lusitania* but had made a last minute change in their plans. The sinking of the *Lusitania* provoked indignation and an eruption of hellfire and brimstone from the religious community. The Reverend L.J. Roderick of Upton Vale viciously attacked the action:

> 'I stood by the bedside of my little boy, who of his own accord (it was the first time I had heard it) prayed "God bless the Germans and God bless the English". How can we reconcile the two? How can we pity that deluded nation and the misguided men who are led blindly into unspeakable wrong, and yet blaze with holy wrath against the deeds which fill the world with horror?...Last August I was convinced that our cause was just. I go further today, it is a crusade and every outrage burns that thought into our soul...I say we are fighting not for our existence, or for the

rights of men; we are fighting for God himself. If Germany wins – this is to me unspeakable, and I will go further impossible – but if Germany wins, it is not the British Empire that will crash into ruins, it is the Church of God that will be swept away. This is not a war with Germany but with Anti-Christ.'

Anti-German riots broke out across the country including in Torquay where Mr Wolff, a naturalised German who owned a shop in St Marychurch, was targeted on 14 May. Having heard rumours of an attack, police were patrolling the area and had to move on a crowd of 300 to 400 who had gathered by Wolff's shop. Unfortunately some of the crowd slipped away and a cry of 'They have done it!' arose with the crowd rushing towards Wolff's shop to find a rock had been thrown through the front window. Fortunately the police presence prevented any greater damage and the crowd was eventually dispersed. The *Directory* described this bout of mob violence as a 'protest against German atrocities' but it was nothing more than a spontaneous outburst of anger and opportunism.

Quickly following the *Lusitania* controversy the Bryce Report on the conduct of the Germans during the invasion of Belgium was published. Coming at a time when negative sentiment had already led to rioting in towns as genteel as Torquay, it roused the country's anger to even greater levels. Sensing the national mood, Prime Minister Asquith announced that all enemy aliens of military age were to be interned and their dependants deported. In Torquay less than a dozen Germans remained. This number reflects how the German community had been decimated thanks to a year of army call-ups, discriminatory laws and anti-German riots. 'Patriot' returned with a letter suggesting that all German place names in the town should be replaced:

> 'Some months ago I called attention to the German names attached to some of the villas and places of which the Town Council have control. I notice that all the names of the villas have since been changed but the council still hang onto the same "Kultur". I suppose they are "keeping down expenses". The dwellers in Brunswick Terrace or Square, would no doubt, take more pride if the word "Mons" met their eyes. "Neuve Chapelle" could very well replace Coburg Place.'

The publication of the Bryce Report was the culmination of a string of German 'atrocities', the invasion of Belgium, the shelling of British towns, Zeppelin raids, the use of gas at Second Ypres and the sinking of the *Lusitania*. It was these events, especially those inflicted upon British citizens, all initiated by the German military, that fuelled the widespread anti-German feeling in Britain. As with the 'rape of Belgium', British propaganda had not lead a docile population into an irrational hatred of the enemy but the enemy's actions had laid the foundation for the hatred that would persist for the rest of the war.

As the fighting on the Western Front intensified so did Torquay's war hospital effort, new figures published showed how April alone had consisted of a fifth of all casualties treated since records began. The increasing contribution of the war hospitals was recognised on 10 September when King George and Queen Mary visited the town to tour the hospitals. It was the king's first visit since reviewing the Royal Navy five years previously.

Torquay Hospital	During April 1915	Since October 1914
Western Hospital	1,653	5,788
Torbay Hospital	1,258	8,731
Rockwood	1,053	4,975
Town Hall Hospital	986	4,125
Total (Number of Men):	4950	23,619

Torquay War Hospitals Usage Since 1914
Source: *TD May 12 1915*

Corporal S. Carwood summed up the town's contributions in the most simple terms, 'You come to Torquay like the sick man of Europe and you go away as healthy and happy as the very Briton himself.' In addition to their role as nurses, women were also finding more opportunities available in late July for the first time in Torquay's history a woman began working as a bank clerk.

By the end of July the first of the Devons' volunteer battalions finally arrived in France. Volunteers had been trickling across the Channel throughout the year but the 8th had suffered a frustrating period in Aldershot earning the mocking title of the 'Aldershot Guards'. One frustrated subaltern wrote in early July 'Have the War Office forgotten us? Are they going to keep us here forever?' He soon got his wish and they left for France on 25 July, quickly joined by their sister battalion the 9th who joined them in 20 Brigade.

Plans for a new offensive were now nearing fruition which involved a combined set of French attacks in Champagne and Artois with the British providing support at the town of Loos. Once again Haig planned for a breakthrough and for the first time he had at his disposal the New Army men, amongst them the Devons. In a belated attempt to maintain some restraint on Haig, French retained control of the reserves and placed them 5,000 to 7,000 yards behind the front line.

About 10pm on 24 September, 20 Brigade was given orders to advance to the front lines. The 8th Devons deployed on the brigade's left with the 2nd Gordons to their right. Behind were the 2nd Borders and the 1/6th Gordons with the 9th Devons in brigade reserve. A Torquinian described the atmosphere:

'We knew we were in for a hot time; but nothing could dampen the spirit of the lads. In the evening, after tea, we had a sing-song – this seems to be the way the evening was spent in most quarters. It will be a long time before that concert is forgotten by the singers...Outside the guns thundered incessantly. As became the lads of Devon the songs were mostly of the Westcountry – songs of home, which for some would tomorrow be beyond ken. This thought was common to all, of course, but it only brought an added sincerity into the dear old songs...Then a grab for rifles, ammunition and equipment, for we were to fall in at 9pm. Thoughts of home and dear ones were thrust aside, and we started on our journey up to the front trenches to prepare for the onslaught on Fritz. Thus did the boys of Devon go into action on that memorable Saturday morning.'

At 5.30am the artillery began, a deluge of shells falling on the enemy trenches with the Germans replying in kind. The British unleashed poison gas and smoke but in places the gas famously blew back into the British trenches. Zero hour was fixed for 6.30am but members of the 8th Devons jumped the gun and began their advance early. They went forward keeping pace with the veteran battalions as they entered battle for the first time. Once they came within sight of the German front line they began to suffer heavy casualties. The subaltern who had been complaining about whether the 8th would ever be sent to the front was amongst the first to fall, alongside him fell many of his fellow officers. A Torquinian wounded in the battle wrote home describing what it was like to have fought that morning:

> 'Six o'clock in the morning came the order: "Prepare to mount the parapet." Well, Bill, we had waited for it for long enough, so up over we went. Talk about hail, our chaps were being bowled over everywhere. By short rushes we go to the first German trench, but very few were left there. Our artillery had hit it to hell. So off to the second one. The firing was deafening. Well, we cleared that trench, Bill, and groped our way to the next one. I say groped, because the gas was affecting us by this time. Anyhow, we cleared that one, and then we lay down. Potting at them, I pulled myself up to get a better sight, when flop, that bullet caught me and knocked me kicking.'

Just after 7am the front line and support line had been taken and the 8th Devons pushed deeper into the German positions; only three officers now remained unwounded but they pressed forward before finally stopping at a crossroads 400 yards west of Hulluch with around seventy-two men remaining. Artillery was still shelling the village and they could go no further despite it being mostly undefended. Furthermore reinforcements weren't forthcoming as the rest of the brigade had taken heavy losses while advancing through areas of unbroken barbed wire. It took until mid-day for the two Devon battalions to join forces with only around fifty men of the 9th remaining to reinforce the 8th as they waited outside Hulluch.

Across the battlefield large areas of barbed wire remained untouched by the artillery, the front had been too large to fully saturate. Although elements broke through, such as the Devons, and the town of Loos was captured, French was slow to release his reserves forcing Haig to use them piecemeal and ineffectively. With the failure to destroy much of the barbed wire and the confusion over reserves, the defenders had time to contain the initial breakthroughs and the offensive ground to a halt. The following day a renewed effort was made. Hastily prepared and without a substantial bombardment it failed with heavy casualties.

After two days of fighting the 8th had lost 639 men including 148 men killed and 129 missing. The 9th fared slightly better with 476 casualties including 59 men killed and 76 missing. Torquay suffered thirteen casualties during the battle including nine on the first day. This made Loos the bloodiest offensive of Torquay's war so far. Many of these men had been volunteers the previous autumn and now lay dead, their bodies strung across no man's land, some hung up on the barbed wire that the artillery had failed to destroy. One Torquinian in the 8th Devons reflected upon the sacrifice made:

'We and all the other regiments who took part paid the price in precious human lives. It is necessary, no one will question that, but the bloodshed, the horror and the pain will remain with us for ever...To the battalions concerned undying credit is due, for every man fought and died like a hero, and never a man faltered or looked back, but all went on, some to their deaths, others right through the German lines of trenches, scattering them like ninepins all the while.

'England may be proud of her sons who lie far away on the fields of France. Those that still live have the awful memory of that ghastly week-end, but look forward to the time when all the death, pain and suffering will be justified by the final crushing of the enemy and the dawn of everlasting peace.'

The battle ground on for another two and a half weeks achieving little. As it continued, Norman Cliff arrived having completed his training and been assigned to the 1st Grenadier Guards. He would now receive his first experience of war:

'Approaching the brow of a hill, we filed into communication trenches that led over the top, and down the slope where exploding shells gave us the first exercise in dodging them. Rain and gunfire had partly demolished the trenches in places, and we were soon scrambling through slush and debris and over the blasted bodies of comrades who had gone ahead of us and met death on the way – a numbing experience for those still living and hoping against hope.

'Leaping into a crumbling concrete maze, in an instant we learned what war – at least this war – was about. Machine guns rattled, bullets were sprayed at us from both flanks, and men fell like skittles in a bowling alley. On all sides grey caps bobbed up – the first Germans we had seen and only a few yards away. Hastily pulling out the pins of our bombs and ignoring the regulation five second delay, we lobbed them inexpertly at the bobbing heads – too hastily, for they came back, blowing several men into lumps of bleeding flesh...We had been living up to our title of Grenadiers – or dying messily if we were unlucky – and earning the right to wear the brass grenade as our cap badge. But it was a high price to pay.'

Shocked by his first experience of war he continues:

'We stumbled back to rest billets, sobered and thoughtful. So this was what was meant by war, a horrifying, nerve stretching initiation, with little gained and all those young lives dissolved in blood.'

Many of the New Army battalions suffered casualties matching or exceeding the Devons. Haig believed that a genuine opportunity had existed for a breakthrough following the capture of Loos and was bitterly disappointed it had not been exploited and soon began to manoeuvre to replace French. Despite the innovations of the year the BEF was still struggling to piece together a successful battle plan. Trench works could now be taken at will but how could they be held? How could the German counter-attacks be defeated? How could the momentum of offensives be sustained? Furthermore as the BEF continued to expand in size, thousands more officers and men would need to be trained, alongside replacing casualties, creating a constant process of training and replacement. The BEF had taken minor steps along the learning curve but there were still many lessons to be learned to prevent another bloody failure like Loos.

The men involved, such as Norman Cliff, were amongst the thousands of volunteers who were now entering the war. This huge outpouring of voluntary recruitment remains unique to this day but by late 1915 it was no longer meeting demand. In a small step towards conscription the government passed the National Registration Act in July requiring all men and women aged between 15 and 65 to report their name and occupation, aiming to establish whether there was still a large pool of manpower that could be tapped by conscription.

The Devons attempted to secure volunteers by marching through Torbay and holding a meeting at Castle Circus where Sergeant Thomas E. Rendle VC claimed that the public should boycott any businesses still employing men of eligible age. Despite this only nine men stepped forward to enlist. The *Torquay Times* pointed out that by its own estimates Torquay had 2,000 men in service, representing 6.5 per cent of its population, a total which it considered more than adequate but despite this the debate on how to encourage more men to enlist continued. Norman Cliff commented upon the feeling about conscription amongst the Guards:

'Wholesale conscription was being urged and the topic cropped up in the billet. Fierce resentment of the slackers found voice, and the general view was that everyone of military age should be called up.'

Despite the debate small-scale enlistment continued; on 13 September another fifteen young men volunteered. By mid-October it was reported that 313 out of the 700 trade unionists in Torquay, hardly a segment of society known for being jingoistic, had signed up. This doesn't seem to have changed opinion amongst those most committed to conscription as Colonel Burn was one of forty MPs who sent a letter to Prime Minister Asquith requesting a meeting to put forward their ideas.

When the National Registration Act returned its findings it showed that 5,012,146 men of military age had yet to enlist and of these only 690,138 were in reserved occupations. To tap into this resource the government initiated what became known as the Derby Scheme. Recruiters would go door-to-door asking men to attest to their willingness to serve. They were then sorted into a number of age groups, where the oldest and those married would be called up later than young single men. Many men who had failed to volunteer had reasons which hadn't changed; an example in Torquay was a young married mechanic who was called upon to serve but who stated that he would only do so if 'my wife and child are adequately looked after' and that 'they cannot be properly provided for by the 14/6 or 15/- per week which would be allowed them'. When told that all men must be prepared to make sacrifices he agreed but replied:

'Would not my wife be making a tremendous sacrifice in letting me go, knowing that I may never return? ...Give me the assurance that my wife and the little one shall be so circumstanced that they can live on the same conditions – or even a *little* less favourable conditions – as they have been living and I will go.'

In some cases men's employers volunteered to make up the shortfall but only the largest companies could afford to do so. While the sons of the wealthy families of the

Lincombes could enlist without financial fear and the poor in Ellacombe could in some cases even benefit from service, many of those of the middle class simply didn't have the option. Despite these issues, the scheme appeared to be spurring those capable of volunteering to head to the recruitment office. A mini boom ensued; over 200 men enlisted during the end of October and beginning of November, an average of between thirty and forty a day. The scheme had been scheduled to end on 30 November but was extended to 11 December as men rushed to volunteer.

In Torquay it was no different, the rush on the final day was tremendous and hundreds of men enlisted, not only from Torquay but also 'Paignton, and still more distant places – Brixham, Totnes, Buckfastleigh, Dittisham, Blackawton and Strete'. A couple of weeks later the initial results were reported: 2,200 men had been interviewed with 800 (36 per cent) pledging to enlist. Roughly 40 per cent of the men interviewed were found to be medically unfit, reflecting the poor diet of many at the time. Although roughly 800 men attesting could be considered a minor success, the scheme was a failure nationwide. Indeed some historians have suggested it was intended to be a failure, paving the way for conscription. In mid-December the cabinet appointed a committee to draft a conscription bill. The days of voluntary enlistment were numbered.

Meanwhile Norman Cliff was experiencing his first winter on the Western Front. On sentry duty he mused to himself:

> 'We had orders to fire an occasional shot and mine might catch someone behind the line. A wave of revulsion overwhelmed me. I couldn't be guilty of it, and not all the officers and NCOs of the British Army would compel me to do it. I would not use my rifle unless there was no alternative...Fritz old boy, what blind insane forces have thrown you and me into this ghastly dilemma?'

He also experienced the unique humour of the trenches:

> 'In quiet moments an exchange of compliments became possible. A voice would shout "How are 'oo Taff?" revealing that the Germans were unaware that we had relieved the Welsh Guards. This was followed swiftly by what sounded like "Hoch der Kaiser!" and swiftly went back "**** the Kaiser and you too!"'

Cliff's experience was typical for the millions who served on the Western Front. From his reminiscences we see an anti-war attitude and a feeling of being abandoned. This view existed but there were also many who displayed more positive views; for many the war was an exciting period in their life and while the conditions were at times horrendous they were proud to be serving their country. There was no one single experience of the Great War and feelings differed depending on where the men were deployed and how much action they saw. If things were as awful as Cliff remembers, why did men such as Guardsman Cliff continue to fight?

No one reason explains why the soldiers put up with such appalling conditions, instead it seems to be a combination of factors. On the side of the stick was punishment: soldiers were subject to strict discipline and a number were shot for desertion throughout the war. Despite being an emotive issue these executions should be put into context. They represented a tiny percentage of the men that served. Only one man was executed in the Devons and many regiments never executed a soldier. There is no documented evidence of a Torquinian being executed during the war. While the threat of court martial was no doubt a restraining influence it was far from as widespread as is sometimes portrayed.

Something which every soldier serving on the Western Front would have experienced was the officer corps. In a society as defined by hierarchy as Edwardian Britain, officers played a huge role in motivating men into combat. A benevolent caring officer could motivate soldiers as much as one barking threats at his men. Furthermore as the war went on and the old officer class became exhausted, increasing numbers of NCOs found their way into the ranks reducing social distance between the men and officers. Far from being distant and uncaring, many officers had made their way through the ranks by the later years of the war and were considered as one of the men even if they were often the subject of grumbling.

In contrast to the sticks were the humdrum daily things that are taken for granted in civilian life. Warm clothing, good accommodation, fresh food, the daily rum ration and rest and relaxation all helped maintain morale. Furthermore soldiers did not spend a prolonged period in the front lines, they were rotated between the front line, reserve trenches and in villages behind the battlefields to recover. There were also the more enjoyable experiences of reading letters from home, watching plays and concerts, playing sports and frequenting the brothels that had sprung up behind the front lines. Newspapers were widespread, the trenches were only a few hundred miles from London and national newspapers could arrive within days of their publication.

There was also a real belief amongst the soldiers that what they were fighting for was right. This was combined with a strong sense of patriotism; the soldiers of the Great War were on the whole patriotic in a way that it is hard to understand from a modern perspective. For many, serving in the trenches was their duty and they would grin and bear the suffering in the name of Britain.

All of these factors combined to help soldiers to survive day to day but there is another factor which is perhaps the most influential in motivating soldiers to fight. This is the idea of 'group identity'. When taken far away from their loved ones, soldiers develop a secondary family. Those sharing the trenches became surrogate brothers and provided emotional support for each other and much needed social contact. When soldiers are interviewed after wars, one of the most cited reasons for why soldiers fight is the intense friendship that is formed in war; in such situations men place themselves in mortal danger in order to protect their comrades.

The final reason for continuing to fight is often overlooked due to its disturbing connotations. This was the enjoyment of war, for many men the experience of being in combat was an exhilarating experience. Corporal Winget commented upon this:

'The sensation of killing a man is not nice, but once done, your blood grows hot, and you seem to see all "red" and a passion unknown in other moments possesses you.'

This combination of fear, anger and exhilaration is often cited by men who have been in battle and while it may not be instrumental in getting men into battle, once the battle has begun it certainly had an effect in motivating some of them.

As the year drew to a close Charles Towell was re-elected as Mayor of Torquay for the fifth year running, making him the longest serving mayor in Torquay's history. News also reached the town that their representative in the French Army, Pierre Brottin, was resting in hospital and recommended for a French Military Medal for bravery. The *Lyons Republican* reported:

> 'On September 25th, a telephone wire being broken, he went out under heavy artillery fire to repair same. On September 26th he repeated the same operation under severe shrapnel and asphyxiating bombardment. Private Brottin is an excellent soldier and very brave.'

In mid-December Sir John French was replaced as Commander-in-Chief of the BEF by Sir Douglas Haig. Although the year's battles had achieved little, Haig had been able to spread a flattering view and where failures had occurred he blamed them upon others such as French's failure to move the reserves forward at Loos. Undoubtedly there was some truth in his arguments, but they also helped to obscure Haig's role. He was as much to blame for the failure throughout 1915 as French but now he was on his own. If the BEF was to ascend the learning curve then it would rely upon Haig coming to grips with the new state of warfare.

Christmas 1915 was a vastly different experience from the previous year. There was a distinctly different feeling amongst the soldiers. Ernst Jünger, a German soldier, wrote in his memoirs that on Christmas Day one of his men was killed:

> 'Immediately after the English attempted a friendly overture and put up a Christmas tree on their parapet. But our fellows were so embittered that they fired and knocked it over. And this in turn was answered with rifle grenades.'

Torquay was far quieter without the boisterous presence of the Dublins, many of whom now lay in shallow graves in the brown dirt of Gallipoli. Indeed no soldiers were billeted in the town over Christmas and over 3,000 Torquinians were celebrating the festive season in places as diverse as Ypres, Cairo and India. The year had cost the lives of at least a further seventy-three local men, sixty-one in the Army and twelve in the Navy, and featured the youngest average age of death during the war at just 26.89 years old, indicative of the loss of many volunteers at Loos. The year had seen the BEF slowly expanding and developing both the tactics and logistical ability to support warfare on a continental scale, fumbling its way along the learning curve. The coming year would see whether it was ready for such a role. The scene was set for escalation.

Chapter 3

1916 - Escalation

'Don't worry, Mother, for God will keep me safe. If it is his holy will that I should be killed, then, dear Mother, you have two consolations; first that I died for my King and Country; secondly, and best of all I died in the grace of God. So don't worry.'
Private Terence Coffey, 19 years old, employed at the Grand Hotel, writing to his mother before going over the top. He died that day.

By early 1916 volunteers were now present in huge numbers and the BEF had finally reached the size where it could conduct offensives by itself. The time had come for Britain to throw its full weight behind the war. The largest British army ever assembled was preparing to go into battle. Clerks, shop keepers, hotel workers, tram operators and others were finding their way to the front lines and learning what was expected of a soldier. One Torquinian wrote home of his early experiences:

'It is surprising how quickly one gets used to the continuous shell fire, and in a few days we reckoned ourselves amongst the cool headed "veterans". One soon learns to distinguish between the shrill note of the light, but dangerous, whizz-bang and the heavier shells known as "coal-boxes" and "Jack Johnsons" used by the Germans and consequently to give them each due respect, according to their proximity to one's dug-out or duty post. It is impossible to run into safety from a shell; the only thing to do is to duck, or even fall flat in the bottom of the trench. This practice soon becomes second nature.'

While many quickly adapted to the living conditions, combat was something quite different. For many it was a horrific, brutalising experience. A corporal in the South Staffords wrote home to his parents in Torquay:

'My word, we had it terrible...The enemy started a great bombardment on February 14th, and kept it up for two days...Our platoon went in with thirty-one men and came out with seven....It was impossible to get them away, as the Huns were dropping their iron foundries as close as could be. They blew in the dressing station and cookhouse, wounding a lot of fellows and killing several. The major came round to us when the Huns tried to cross and said , "Don't forget that you are all Staffords men, and give it to them dxxxxd hot". He was wounded twice, and still kept up, until at last he had to be taken to a dressing station.

'I dressed one poor lad whom I shall never forget. He was hit with a trench mortar that blew half his leg off. I bandaged him, and spent nearly five hours with him, whilst the enemy was pelting us with shells; all the time he was crying out for morphia. The shells came over like throwing corn to fowls, but for all their "strafing" we kept them back...Well, I can tell you I prayed as I never prayed before. I was expecting my tap every minute. Once I had my head against the parapet, and a piece of iron just grazed the peak of my cap. It made me hold my breath and I said "Thank God for that" and I spent the remainder of the time laid on my stomach…It was awful.'

If the British were suffering then the French were about to enter hell. Falkenhayn, having decided that a breakthrough on the Western Front was no longer possible, had decided to bleed France white instead. The place where he chose to do it was the fortress town of Verdun. On the morning of 21 February, 1,220 German guns fired two million shells in eight hours before the German conscripts launched themselves over their parapets. Amongst the unfortunate Frenchmen defending Verdun was Pierre Brottin, once more in the thick of things. For the British, the slaughter around Verdun would mean that the forthcoming offensive, previously planned as a joint offensive, became primarily British; a token French force would remain but the forthcoming battle would now be directed by the BEF.

On the Home Front the government had finally relented and introduced the Military Service Act calling for the conscription of all single men aged between 18 and 41. The Act allowed those who were called up to appeal to a local tribunal, where they could be exempted from service if they had a reasonable excuse or were conscientious objectors. The Act fundamentally changed the way recruitment worked; previously volunteers could choose the regiment they wished to join, now recruits were to be sent to central training depots and allocated to regiments in need of reinforcement. The first group of Torquay recruits under the Derby Scheme had left in late January with the majority choosing to serve in the Devons; conscripted men would have no choice. This created a situation where a Torquinian could find himself serving in a regiment as remote as the Argyll and Sutherland Highlanders, however Torquay would retain an influence in the Devons until the end of the war.

It didn't take long for the exemption for conscientious objectors to cause controversy. The *Torquay Times* viciously attacked it:

'This clause has created a greater difficulty than ever. It has induced a number of persons – it would hardly be fair to our brave fellows to call them "men" – to discover that they possessed a tender "conscience" which prevented them from "doing their bit" as fellow citizens in this national crisis. The answers given by these "jelly-fish" objectors at some at the tribunals are amazing…They are to form a special "Non-Combatant Corps."…The NCC's want to save their skins, but they will be flayed alive with ridicule.'

Such language seems incredible today but the *Torquay Times* wasn't being particularly radical in its views. In a less than subtle attempt to prevent appeals, it also began printing accounts of the meetings of the Torquay tribunal. The first meeting extensively covered was in late January and consisted of a number of aldermen and an army representative, Colonel Stovell, who harangued the appellants.

The cases varied vastly including a 19-year-old assistant manager at a local dairy, a partner of a local toy company who had been attempting to 'capture' the German toy trade and a multi-talented man who described himself as 'a pig dealer, haulier and teacher of music'. The majority of appeals were based upon the assertion that being conscripted would financially affect the conscripted man, with illness being a distant second. Most men were given extensions to their call-ups, commonly for a month or two.

Contrary to the controversy about conscientious objectors, only three men out of twenty-two came forward under those terms. Frank Tucker, 27, a greengrocer's porter claimed conscientious objection. A representative of his employer stated that if the Army took him 'he did not think he would be kept a month'. When asked whether he wanted to go to war, Frank replied, 'I don't want anything to do with it...I hate war.' The tribunal decided that Frank needed to acquire a certificate from an Army doctor to prove his 'religious mania', in which case he would be exempt from service.

This early case suggests little evidence of the abuse of the system that the media suggested was rife. Many of the men who appealed, did so due to a fear of what might happen to their families. While it could be argued that a fear of war was hidden behind economic arguments, the majority of those citing economic reasons had valid reasons for their appeal.

The statistics tell an interesting story: of 197 men recorded, 94.2 per cent were successful in delaying signing up, the vast majority citing financial reasons. The table shows that 48.22 per cent of all appeals resulted in a limited exemption from call-up due to economic circumstances, the actual number is probably significantly higher given the number of men whose reasons were not stated.

Regarding conscientious objectors, none were exempted from service in this period and only four were given non-combative roles. As a percentage of total appeals they numbered only 2 per cent. This figure is broadly in line with other municipalities, such as Huddersfield which recorded less than 1 per cent from this group in 1916. It is clear that in early 1916 conscientious objection was not widespread in Torquay. What is perhaps most surprising is that 94.2 per cent of all appeals were successful in gaining some kind of exemption. Colonel Stovell objected to the large number of appeals granted but the rest of the tribunal retorted that they were merely following advice from government. However only 5.08 per cent of appeals were rejected, compared to a figure of 24.5 per cent in Huddersfield for 1916. This suggests that perhaps the Torquay tribunal was unduly lenient despite the fact that appeal rejections naturally increased after the Somme, hence Huddersfield's significantly larger figure.

Reason for Appeal	Number of Appeals	Percentage of Total Appeals
Exemption From Service For A Limited Time Period		
Economic Reasons	95	48.22%
Health Reasons	5	2.54%
Conscientious Objection	0	0%
War Work	5	2.54%
Unstated Reasons	50	25.38%
Total / Percentage of Total Appeals	155	78.68%

Reason for Appeal	Number of Appeals	Percentage of Total Appeals
Total Exemption From Service Granted		
Economic Reasons	9	4.57%
Health Reasons	8	4.06%
Conscientious Objection	0	0%
Unstated Reasons	10	5.08%
Total / Percentage of Total Appeals	27	13.71%
Exemptions From Combative Service		
Economic Reasons	0	0%
Health Reasons	1	0.51%
Conscientious Objection	4	2.03%
Unstated Reasons	0	0%
Total / Percentage of Total Appeals	5	2.54%
Rejection of Appeal		
Didn't Attest Under Derby Scheme	1	0.51%
Conscientious Objection	0	0%
Appealed Too Late	2	1.02%
Denied Extension of Exemption	1	0.51%
Soldier Wished To Sign Up	1	0.51%
No Case To Be Argued	3	1.52%
Unstated Reasons	2	1.02%
Total / Percentage of Total Appeals	10	5.08%
Total Number of Successful Appeals	187	94.2%
Total Number of Rejected Appeals	10	5.08%
Total Number of Appeals	197	

Documented Appeals to Torquay Military Service Tribunal from inception to the Battle of the Somme, 1916
Source: *Torquay Times* reports of Military Service Tribunals, February 25 1916 to 7 July 1916 (inclusive).

Economically, both the country and the town were struggling. On February 18 an advert appeared in the *Torquay Times* asking its readers to give a standing order to their newsagents as 'few if any' copies would be printed for chance sales due to the paper shortage. The price of bread in the town had increased to 9d for the quarter loaf compared to 5¹/₂d before the war. There were, however, some economic rays of light. The Marine Spa opened in front of roughly a thousand people and a movie based on the novel *Beau Brocade* was being filmed by the Lucoque Company in Cockington, with a cast of twenty-two, one of whom was allegedly a leading actress, but these bright spots were few and far between. On 2 May the Military Service Act was extended to married men and in the middle of the month the last of the married men who had signed up under the Derby scheme departed.

So far in 1916 the British front had been comparatively quiet as Germany fixed her gaze upon Verdun. Around the Ypres Salient, Plumer was engaged in a number of small operations but foul weather affected his ability to do much of worth. He had been working on plans for a breakout from the Ypres Salient and had expanded trench raiding as a result. At the forefront were the ANZACs, who having arrived from Gallipoli now made up almost a third of his army. Plumer had a strong relationship with them as shown by a soldier calling out in the night to a passing Australian battalion, 'Where are you off to Aussie?' and receiving the reply, 'We don't know, but thank God we're going to Daddy Plumer's Army.' When a number of the Australian divisions later headed to the Somme they were reported as singing 'Take me back to Daddy Plumer's Army.' The transfer of the Australians was typical of the year for Plumer as he held on and provided reinforcements for the Somme, receiving in return the worn-out remnants of battalions.

With Plumer holding the shattered remains of Ypres and the preparation for the Somme continuing, attention now turned to a theatre of war that had been largely forgotten. The North Sea had been quiet aside from a small engagement at Dogger Bank but around 600 Torquinians were now serving in the navy. This lack of activity soon changed as the British and German Fleets clashed at the Battle of Jutland. The battle was fought throughout the second half of May 31 and into the early hours of June 1. It was a confusing and inconclusive battle although arguably a British strategic victory as it maintained the British Navy's dominance of the North Sea for the rest of the war. Heavy casualties were suffered on both sides with British casualties numbering over 6,000.

Amongst the British ships lost that day were HMS *Indefatigable*, onboard which twelve Torquinians died and HMS *Queen Mary*, where four more lost their lives. Seaman Endcott, an old schoolboy of Upton School, on-board HMS *Dublin* and heavily involved in the fighting described the battle as 'a terrible experience, a rain of shells, unearthly noises, flame and smoke'.

The first Torquay heard of the battle was on 2 June. The *Directory* claimed that 'sounds of mourning were heard in Torre and other parts of the town when it became known that the ships had disappeared and that few men had been saved.' As more information filtered in, families from Wellswood to Ellacombe began to receive news of the loss of their loved ones. At least twenty-nine Torquinians lost their lives during Jutland, far surpassing the toll at Coronel. Although later offensives on the Western Front would be worse, Jutland was the bloodiest single day in Torquay's history until the bombings of the Second World War. Never again would so many local men give their lives on a single day in defence of king and country. The national myth of the war has elevated the first day of the Somme above all other events, however for Torquay and other coastal communities Jutland was as devastating and should be remembered to a greater extent than it is.

With the German Navy checkmated, attention turned once more to the Somme.

Much of the preparation was complete. The divisions of the BEF had been training strenuously for months, battle plans had been formulated, huge supply dumps had been gathered, detailed reconnaissance of the German lines had been carried out and there were rumours of a surprise new weapon. Everything was ready for the 'Big Push' and it was desperately needed. The French at Verdun needed urgent relief. Pierre Brottin, representing Torquay amongst his Gallic comrades, had suffered alongside his nation and been invalided to a hospital after suffering shell wounds in the head and a severe wound to the chest.

The middle day of the middle year of the war: 1 July, a date forever seared into Britain's consciousness. On a battlefield straddling the River Somme, the New Armies deployed en masse.

The Somme was a huge battle and to cover the entirety in a book of this size would be impossible. To understand the experience of the Somme through Torquay's eyes, three battalions will be followed. They are the 2nd Devons, the Regular battalion still containing a number of Torquinians, and the 8th and 9th Devons, the New Army battalions containing large numbers of volunteer Torquinians. For those interested in learning more about the Devons during this day, the Channel 4 documentary 'The Somme' (2006) heavily features the actions of the 2nd Devons and is a good place to start.

The battle was preceded by an artillery bombardment previously unsurpassed, over 1.5 million shells were fired in a week long bombardment. Serving amongst the artillerymen, Percy Fawcett remarked the battle was nothing less than 'Armageddon'. The BEF had misread the lessons of 1915 and instead of organising intense hurricane bombardments decided upon a prolonged bombardment, the expectation being that nothing would remain standing. The problem was that such a prolonged bombardment gave the Germans plenty of time to prepare. Orders were given for a slow and orderly walking advance such was the belief in the artillery and also the worry that lack of experience amongst the volunteers would hinder any complex orders.

The 2nd Devons as part of the 8th Division had been assigned the objective of taking the village of Ovillers, located roughly in the centre of the battlefield and directly east of their trenches. At 6.35am a huge bombardment opened, the last before the battle. The Devons had been assembled in their trenches since the previous evening and the silent waiting must have been dreadful. At 7.25am the forward companies scrambled over the parapet. All along the front thousands of men were doing the same. When the artillery barrage moved forward, advanced elements were only 100 yards away from the German trenches. It was as far as many of them reached. German soldiers, scrambling up from their largely undamaged bunkers, manned their machine guns and began strafing the approaching men.

The impact of this opening enfilade was immense. Men fell in heaps all around the German front line. As the rear companies of the Devons arrived into the killing zone they crashed into the stumbling remnants of their comrades and they too suffered the same fate. A few brave men made it into the German trenches but they quickly joined their comrades as casualties. Those lucky souls that found some cover were pinned down, many wounded, as machine-gun fire strafed the blood splattered ground in front of them. There they remained, crouching in shell holes until the artillery bombardment returned to the German front lines around mid-day allowing the wounded to crawl back to safety. Those seriously wounded and unable to move bled out their lives in agony until they died.

The battalion was crippled, suffering 431 casualties including 232 killed or missing. Amongst the losses were four Torquinians, Augustine Hannaford, Ernest John Hatton, Leo Jacob Langwasser and Joseph Tanner.

The Somme front was bisected by a road running from Albert to Bapaume, to the north of it where the 2nd Devons had been deployed; the attack was an unmitigated disaster, however to the south the BEF achieved more success. The 8th and 9th Devons were located in the centre of the southern front, a few miles down the line from the 2nd. Their objective was the village of Mametz, located directly north. The 9th were to attack in the initial assault with the 8th as battalion reserve. At 7.27am, two minutes later than their comrades further north the 9th left their trenches. The advance went well until the men arrived at Mansel Copse, an area dominated by a machine-gun position, the right flank of the 9th was enfiladed and many men fell. The left flank achieved more success and was soon amongst the German front lines.

The artillery had been much more effective in this sector and the barbed wire had been effectively cut, even if the German trenches were typically undamaged. Despite this, strong German resistance slowed down the 9th's advance and it soon turned into a violent series of back and forth trench assaults. At 10.30am the 8th advanced to support their comrades. Passing Mansel Copse, they encountered the same issues and within minutes the advance company lost its commanding officer and all other officers had been hit. Order was soon restored and the men advanced into the trenches where they too met heavy resistance. Early afternoon was spent in bloody hand-to-hand fighting as the battalions bludgeoned and bombed their way forwards towards Mametz, which was taken by early evening, and across the southern front comparable gains were being made.

Despite this relative success, losses were still heavy. The 9th lost 463 casualties out of 775 men, a casualty rate of 60 per cent, including 141 men killed and 55 missing; of its officers, only one remained unwounded. The 8th, advancing into less resistance, still lost 49 men killed and missing. Amongst the dead were five Torquinians, Edward John Basset and William Browning of the 8th and William Owen Mayers and Sidney Hooper Fedrick and William Orsman of the 9th.

Three days later, at Mansel Copse where many of the 8th and 9th had fallen, a piece of land was cleared and a cemetery was created. That evening 160 men were buried at the site and a special service was held. All of the Torquinians were buried at Devonshire Cemetery and remain there to this day. To complete the cemetery a makeshift wooden board was nailed in place with the famous inscription:

'The Devonshires held this trench. The Devonshires hold it still.'

The relative success of the southern front can be explained by a number of factors, the artillery bombardment was far more effective, cutting barbed wire and doing more damage. It had been woefully inadequate in sectors such as the 2nd Devons' with many shells failing to explode and those that did doing little damage. Many of the divisions in the south were better trained, commanders had moved their soldiers into no man's land early and ignored the infamous walking orders. Contrary to the myth, none of the Devons walked across the Somme. Finally the proximity of the French, further to the south, helped the advance, their tactics were far superior and they had achieved all of their objectives on the first day.

The BEF had suffered 57,470 casualties including 19,240 killed, the worst single day losses in the British Army's history. Torquay witnessed first-hand the results of the battle when 125 wounded soldiers arrived in the first week of the offensive. The first day affected the town relatively less than the industrialised cities, the lack of a Pals battalion meant it escaped the casualty figures of towns such as Accrington and Bradford, nevertheless at least fifteen Torquinians died on 1 July. It was the town's second bloodiest day after Jutland and would not be forgotten quickly.

Despite these losses the BEF quickly learned from its mistakes. The walking orders would never be repeated, the importance of devolving decisions was recognised, as was the element of surprise and the need for more effective artillery barrages. Haig and his subordinates had blundered and should be held accountable for the bloodshed, but they soon began altering their methods.

Although remembered for the first day, the battle dragged on for nearly four and a half months and turned into a bloody attritional stuggle. On the second day, one of Torquay's great landed families lost a son when Lawrence Palk, the second son of Lord Haldon, was killed. Another local notable, Colonel Lucius Cary the owner of Torre Abbey, slipped away peacefully at home shortly after. His estate passed to Lieutenant Lancelot Cary, who was also fighting on the Somme. Cary just had enough time to jot down a reply to the Borough Council's letter of condolence as he sheltered in his trench. He wrote: 'Please excuse short scrappy letter, but when I tell you I am writing under heavy shell fire you will understand. My battalion has been and still is engaged in heavy fighting.' By the time his letter had been printed on 26 July he was dead, the second Cary to die within a month. A Torquinian, Lance-Corporal Harris, witnessed Cary's last moments:

> 'Mr Cary led A Company through a large wheat field straight towards the German line, and when we got fairly close to it a machine gun opened fire on us. Mr Cary gave the signal to drop and take cover, and was shot through the head whilst doing so.'

The death duties inflicted upon the Cary estate by the deaths of two of its members crippled the already struggling family. Lieutenant Cary's heir, Captain Lionel Cary, struggled to pay the family debts and by 1930 his son was forced to sell Torre Abbey to the town council.

What is often called the Battle of the Somme actually consisted of a number of battles following each other. The first was the Battle of Albert and as that ground to a halt attention turned to the Battle of Bazentin Ridge. It was to be made on the southern front where the BEF had experienced its few successes so far, meaning that the 8th and 9th Devons were to go back into action. They had previously captured the first line of German trenches and they were now to face the second and third. Planning took account of the lessons of 1 July, battalions were sent into no man's land the previous evening and lay in wait, ready to rush the Germans after the bombardment ended and the prolonged barrage was swapped for a five-minute blitz giving the defenders no time to react.

As the Devons waited silently for the guns to begin, one Devonian officer of the 8th recalled his thoughts:

> 'Could the silence last until the hurricane bombardment of five minutes was due to start? 3am all quiet; 3.05 all quiet; 3.10 only a few of our MGs doing overhead fire in a casual way; 3.15 a few stray shells, but nothing to denote an alarm; 3.18; 3.19; 3.20! Then every gun for miles around gave tongue as the shells hurtled overhead. The surprise had succeeded!'

The Devons stormed forward and were soon clearing out the German trenches. The fight on their right flank was stiffer but they overcame it and by 4am had taken their initial objectives, by mid-afternoon all objectives had been taken. The 9th Devons hadn't even needed to be involved. Total casualties were 171 men for the 8th and 90 for the 9th who had caught a blow from the German counter-barrage. For a brief moment breakthrough loomed but tardiness in bringing cavalry forward meant that by the early evening the Germans had sufficiently recovered to prevent any further gains. This failure to exploit the opportunity repeated the pattern of the war so far but contrary to the myth of poor generalship, Bazentin Ridge had shown real tactical improvement. This is reflected in the significantly lower casualty rates amongst the 8th and 9th Devons. There is no documented evidence of a Torquinian death on that day. The opportunity for a breakthrough may have been lost but just two weeks after 1 July, the BEF continued climbing the learning curve.

The shocking losses of the first day resulted in changes at the military service tribunals. Unfortunately the sources available for the second half of the year are far fewer, newspapers began cutting down on their coverage, partly because there was less need to shame men. With only around a third of the sample size it's harder to come to decisive conclusions but a few trends appear. Economic motives were still the primary motivation for appealing and despite the disaster on the Somme the number of conscientious objectors only increased from four in the first half of the year to five. However if we assume that the pattern in these sixty-six men was repeated in the undocumented appeals and multiply the number by three to give a similar sample size to the first half of the year, this produces fifteen men or roughly 7.5 per cent of appeals, a rise from the 2.03 per cent of the first six months. Clearly the news filtering across the Channel was having an effect, however the total was not exceptionally high. Finally total exemptions and exemptions from military service remained largely stable although rejections of appeals doubled from 5.08 per cent to 10.61 per cent representing the need to get men into uniform. With the limited data available it can be suggested that the Somme had a minor effect upon views of the war, however the primary motivation for appeal remained economic.

Reason for Appeal	Number of Appeals	Percentage of Total Appeals

Exemption From Service For A Limited Time Period

Economic Reasons	38	57.58%
Health Reasons	6	9.09%
Conscientious Objectors	2	3.03%
War Work	1	1.52%
Unstated Reasons	1	1.52%
Total / Percentage of Total Appeals	*48*	*72.73%*

Total Exemption From Service Granted

Economic Reasons	5	7.58%
Health Reasons	0	0%
War Work	4	6.06%
Conscientious Objectors	0	0%
Unstated Reasons	0	0%
Total / Percentage of Total Appeals	*9*	*13.64%*

Exemptions From Combative Service

Economic Reasons	0	0%
Health Reasons	0	0%
Conscientious Objection	2	3.03%
Unstated Reasons	0	0%
Total / Percentage of Total Appeals	*2*	*3.03%*

Rejection of Appeal

Conscientious Objection	1	1.52%
No Case To Be Argued	4	6.06%
German Ancestry	1	1.52%
Health	1	1.52%
Unknown	0	0%
Total / Percentage of Total Appeals	*7*	*10.61%*

Total Number of Successful Appeals	*59*	*89.39%*
Total Number of Rejected Appeals	*7*	*10.61%*
Total Number of Appeals	*66*	

Appeals to Torquay Military Service Tribunal, July to December 1916
Source: *Torquay Times* reports of Military Service Tribunals, 14 July 1916 to end of year.

Back on the Somme failure to capitalise on previous successes meant the BEF had become involved in increasingly bloody attritional actions. Lessons were still not being universally applied and large losses were being suffered, but now Haig had a new trick up his sleeve – the tank.

Torquinian Norman Cliff had now arrived on the Somme and rumours were circulating that a new weapon was to be deployed. Cliff had heard vague talk about a secret weapon but was unaware of its exact nature. The Battle of Flers-Courcelette was the opening of the final general offensive of the Somme on 15 September. Despite impressive first day results, once again the battle soon ran out of momentum, only nine out of forty-nine tanks deployed managed to reach the German front lines. The soldiers' view of this new 'secret weapon' can be seen in Cliff's reflections:

'Where was the secret weapon? We had been excited by vague rumours of a formidable new machine that would scare the Germans out of their wits, and spread panic all along the line. The first troops to attack had been preceded by a creeping barrage which left gaps 100ft wide for the terror machine – but none arrived in our sector. It appears that nine were allotted, two had engine trouble and came too late, and the rest lost direction and wandered aimlessly about.'

Another Torquinian wrote home with a slightly more favourable view:

'We forced the blighters to take shelter in their dug-outs and then we started blasting them out with bombs and digging them out with bayonets. It was a hot strafe and no mistake. They have as many tricks as monkeys, but we kept ferreting them out until the last batch were rounded up…Some said it was the sight of the 'land dreadnoughts' that had done it. Perhaps it was. More likely it was the rocking of the ground under our fire.'

Despite the failure to achieve a breakthrough, the German lines were broken into once more and the front line advanced. For Torquay it was another bloody episode with five Torquinians falling on 15 September. By the end of the Battle of Flers-Courcelette and its sequel, the Battle of Morval, much of the German trench network on the Somme had now been captured but it had cost hundreds of thousands of casualties on both sides. German morale was beginning to flag. Cliff came across this when dealing with German PoWs:

'The German team sprang to their feet, threw up their hands and came forward led by a young officer with an Iron Cross dangling from his chest. Automatically we lowered our rifles and the officer held out his hand, and in English asked us to accept their surrender. "Where did you learn your English," I asked. "In London where I worked," he replied. I was struck by his dignity in a desperate situation, and there was no question of butchering them. Realising that he and his team were to be spared, he burst out, addressing me "You've been so decent to us that I would like to present you with this," indicating his Iron Cross. "No! You must have done something fine to get it, and I wouldn't dream of taking it from you."'

In late September Cliff was wounded and was invalided home to a hospital in Liverpool, where he spent the next nine and a half months recovering. He was one of the lucky ones. By mid-November the battle finally stumbled to a halt. The BEF had at its furthest point advanced seven miles, roughly the distance from Torquay to Newton Abbot town centres.

The Somme offensive cost Torquay at least sixty-nine men killed, probably more. It was the bloodiest campaign of the war for the town. Losses had been extremely heavy and some communities had been devastated, however at the time it was seen as a necessary battle and the Torquay media reported along these lines. Its modern legacy is heavily debated between those who view it as a bloody waste and those who view it as a necessary step on the learning curve towards defeating Germany.

Before the attack began, the BEF was a collection of divisions largely untested in battle and its generals had little experience of war on this scale. While it is true that 1 July was a disaster, lessons were soon learned. The BEF quickly adapted, introducing more efficient counter-battery work, advancing into no man's land the evening before an assault, delegating more command power to those on the spot and introducing new weapons such as the tank. By late November the BEF had been transformed, its rank and file becoming hardened soldiers, no longer clerks and tram conductors. Haig and others were still guilty of continuing offensives long beyond the chance of a breakthrough had passed but they were improving and by the end of the year, the BEF little resembled the force of 1 July. As it grew in strength its enemy was weakening; the Somme combined with Verdun, which had finally ended in mid-December, cost the German Army many of its veterans and significantly weakened its manpower; in the coming year increasing numbers of inexperienced young men would be called up.

As the BEF was heavily engaged in the Battle of Flers-Courcelette, Torquay joined the rest of the country in flocking to the cinema to watch the latest sensation, the film 'The Battle of the Somme' which was being shown at the Electric Theatre. The film had been shot that summer during the early stages of the battle and was surprisingly graphic. For many citizens of Torquay this would have been their most realistic experience of the war so far. Still at the cinema, on 31 September the town experienced its first 'Round-Up', a draconian action organised to catch men who had deserted or were actively avoiding conscription. Patrons of the Electric Theatre were 'somewhat startled' when the lights were raised in the middle of a film and a policeman appeared and told all the men present that they must provide their papers. Upwards of a hundred men were forced to remain behind and produce personal details. The *Torquay Times* noted that because of a munition workers' holiday a large number of men were in possession of 'badges' exempting them from the draft and thus the round-up was a failure.

The voracious appetite of the war was also beginning to impinge upon people's daily living standards. Prices had steadily risen and, as inevitably happens during war, some crafty people had spied an opportunity of making a few extra pounds. Fish, the one staple food which should have been relatively simple to come by, experienced a bout of war profiteering with mackerel being sold on Torquay harbour for 'a little over a penny' but for 4d in shops a short walk up the high street. The increasing cost of these basic necessities made life tough in Torquay, whose main industry had been damaged by the war. There was one bright piece of economic news as the year came to an end: Torquay continued its role as a garrison town with the arrival of the 1/4th to 4/4th Battalions of the London Regiment.

On 7 December, Prime Minister Asquith finally resigned and was replaced by David Lloyd-George. The past year had been a turning point, shattering any myths that remained about war. The most obvious and long lasting effect upon Torquay was the death of 143 men, more than the previous years combined, the average age of fallen Torquinians just 28.23 years old. Yet despite these problems there remained a desire to finish the job, Germany must be defeated, no matter the cost. The Somme had shocked the public but it had not defeated their fighting spirit. Elsewhere little had changed and the two warring alliances remained deadlocked. It was becoming increasingly obvious that one factor above all would decide who would emerge victorious. Endurance.

Chapter 4

1917 - Endurance

*'Gentlemen, we may not make history tomorrow, but we will certainly
change the geography.'*
- General Herbert Plumer, before the Battle of Messines

As the fourth year of the war began victory seemed as far away as ever, however Verdun and the Somme had inflicted heavy losses upon the Germans. Falkenhayn had been replaced by Hindenburg and Ludendorff, and the German forces withdrew to a new defensive position known as the Hindenburg Line. This shortened their lines by 30 miles and gifted the Allies all the territory they had fought over during 1916 without a major battle.

During 1917 Ludendorff and Hindenburg would remain on the defensive in the west while they attempted to defeat Russia. Back in London, Lloyd George had finally committed Britain to a full mobilisation of the home front and, after spending 1916 holding the frontline at Ypres, Herbert Plumer was about to enter his defining year of the war at Messines and Passchendaele. In these battles and others, the rapidly improving BEF would bear the brunt of the Allied war effort.

As the armed forces pulled ever more men into their orbit, small provincial towns such as Torquay represented a useful reservoir of labour. Throughout January and February the press featured a multitude of advertisements encouraging those not already serving to relocate to the Midlands to work in the munitions factories as the home front mobilised to support the insatiable demand for shells, bullets and rifles. As Torquay's male population disappeared the 1/4th to 4/4th battalions of the London Regiment had been garrisoned in the town and integrated well, if never reaching the popularity of the Dublins. More illustrious guests were also present including the former King of Portugal, Manuel II.

The financial strains upon Torquay continued to grow; in early February the council took out a bank loan of £50,000 to invest into the War Loan and used some of the money to pay employees earning £150 a year or less a 10 per cent war bonus. With prices constantly rising and the economic health of the town worsening this money was vital to those that received it, but the poor of Pimlico and Ellacombe were given no help. The citizens of Torquay also donated to the War Loan, managing to raise the substantial sum of £2m, beating Exeter which raised only £1.35m. Torquay's war loan contribution was the largest in Devon per capita at £50 with Exeter raising just £22 10s and Plymouth only £12.

On 1 February the policy of unrestricted submarine warfare was resurrected in an effort to starve Britain out of the war. Ludendorff and Hindenburg knew that this would bring the United States into the war but decided that it was an acceptable risk in exchange for defeating Britain. It did not take long for the effects of this decision to reach Torquay. At midnight on 20 March, the hospital ship *Asturias* was torpedoed without warning. The ship sank, the majority of the ship's passengers escaping in lifeboats, but many were lost at sea. Twenty-four bodies from the wreck came ashore in Torquay. The impact of bodies appearing in the harbour was a shocking event. The anger felt was even greater given the dead were supposed to have been under the protection of the Red Cross.

The sinking of the *Asturias* was one of hundreds of incidents that occurred that spring as the U-boats wreaked havoc. In April alone 800,000 tons of shipping was sunk and one quarter of all ships that left British ports failed to return. At the height of the crisis only six weeks of food remained in Britain. It was only a matter of time before such losses would force Britain out of the war. As the home front teetered on the edge, the United States finally declared war upon Germany. The *Torquay Times* reacted positively:

'America at last is coming over the parapet. After a long time of patient deliberation she has committed herself to a deliberate act...Germany as well as others, have asked "What can America do?" They will know very soon, America will be no passive spectator. She will enter the war with all the hustle and ingenuity of her clever race. She has a population of a hundred million and wealth unlimited. Men, money and munitions are the three requisites wanted to win the war...Now we have our assurance made doubly sure that Germany cannot win the war, nor her U-boats starve us out.'

Overnight the war had changed. Victory would come down to whether the British public could survive until the Americans arrived in France. The war was inching towards a conclusion but submarine attacks continued throughout the year. The Brixham trawling fleet was regularly attacked by U-boats and in one bad week six vessels were lost. With this action occurring literally over the horizon, Torquay was under siege.

As on the Home Front, the first half of the year brought only bad news for the BEF. In early March Tsar Nicholas II was toppled from power and Russian support could no longer be relied upon. In France, the German withdrawal had totally surprised the Allied forces. Second Lieutenant Ernest Brown, a Torquinian, described the scene left behind: 'Utter desolation prevailed. Everything of value had either been taken away or destroyed.'

The year had not begun auspiciously, however the latest French attack, the 'Nivelle Offensive', was about to be launched. The British contribution was a subsidiary attack on the town of Arras, designed to draw German reserves away from the main French assault. When Ernest Brown arrived he would quickly realise that lessons of the Somme had been learned.

The Battle of Arras, fought from 9 April to 16 May was a more limited engagement than the Somme; the artillery bombardment was twice as intense; new '106' fuses had been manufactured in large quantities and exploded upon impact destroying barbed wire; creeping barrages and more efficient counter-battery work were widely used; gas was deployed and tanks used more effectively. The result of these tactical and material improvements was that although the Battle of Arras involved almost as many soldiers as the first day of the Somme, casualties in the first three days of the battle were fewer than half those of the opening phase of the Somme and a three and a half mile advance was made.

Lessons learned were being put into action but unfortunately, after the first day, the usual pattern of prolonging the battle was repeated and the offensive ground down into a stalemate. It was drained of its vigour by the new German doctrine of 'elastic defence' where front line trenches were sparsely occupied, leaving soldiers safe from artillery bombardment and free to counter-attack more efficiently. Arras cost a further twenty-one Torquinian casualties.

To the south, the Nivelle Offensive was an utter failure and the French Army finally snapped. Widespread mutinies and desertion broke out, regiments refused to return to the trenches and nearly half the French Army experienced some form of disruption. The French would be incapable of any large-scale offensive operations for a number of months.

In the war against Turkey, Baghdad had now been captured but two British attempts to break out of Egypt were defeated. The British would be stuck outside Gaza for the next few months as they awaited reinforcements, amongst them the 1/5th Devons, still containing a number of Torquinians and finally departing India. During the skirmishes around Gaza, A.B. Dale, who had previously written home about his distaste of Egypt, was on top form once again writing about the fighting in an odd but enthralling style:

'Khaki on our side, and grey green on theirs, is certainly a fair show of colour for any man with ambitious hopes of becoming a King's shot. Hours of this go on, and presently an opportunity is afforded, and away the Light Horse go riding for dear life or cheap death towards the enemy. The young man's feelings at this particular period were all in all for the possibility of riding down that "Fez" that persisted in showing "red", a dangerous colour at any time. Well, his hopes are attained, he is on him, he rides him down, and is another twenty yards onwards before he reaches him....

'Two more Johnny Turks are ahead. More spree. One turns and fires, the bullet ricocheting from the stirrup iron into the sand. (One flag for a miss). The other, who is on the left turns half round, and the young man finishes his turn to a whole, with his sword, but minus his head. The other meanwhile, has not been idle, and at about 10 yards distance aims point blank at the young man, and pulls the trigger. The next few seconds and his right arm is off at the shoulder. How about the young man? Was he killed? Oh no for the reason that that particular Turk was the same man who had fired previously and hit the stirrup iron, and unfortunately for him, and fortunately for the young man, had forgotten to reload his one-chambered rifle.

'A few more bouts, and the young man, swigging a drink of damnably hot water from his water bottle, has a look round. He spies but one other Australian about. Where are the others? Somewhere in the numerous hollows that abound? Perhaps? Oh well, he joins hands with the other horseman and makes tracks to re-join the troops. Bad luck! There is no sign of the troop or other horsemen. Suddenly in a hollow, some Turkish stragglers appear. They are killed. Why? Because the "we saw them first" game was in our favour.'

Gaza and other less well known fronts were a world away from France but formed a significant part of the experience of the war for many Torquinians, witnessing as much bravery and sacrifice as their more famous counterparts.

The mental demands the Army placed upon its soldiers were in many ways as great as the physical and by 1917 there began to emerge in Torquay cases of soldiers suffering from shell shock, what we'd now call post-traumatic stress disorder. Percy Fawcett appeared to be suffering from some form of it. When he visited home on leave, he often sat for hours without speaking, holding his head in his hands. For some the thought of being forced to go to war was enough to traumatise them. In early February Private Leonard Cohen of the Londons was sitting near the Princess Pier when he noticed a figure approach the railings and look over the edge. The man took off his hat and coat before clambering over and throwing himself into the water. Cohen dashed onto the pier and threw a lifebuoy into the water but the man refused to grab it. At this point Private Marlor, also of the Londons, rushed to Cohen's aid but the man still refused their help and disappeared under the water. His name was Frank Tucker, the same Frank Tucker who had appeared at the town's first tribunal claiming conscientious objection.

At the inquest into Tucker's death, his employer stated that Tucker had recently been ordered to report to the tribunal again and was in an anxious state. Customers asked him about his visit and Tucker had exclaimed 'they will never have me'. After hearing the evidence the coroner ruled a verdict of suicide whilst in a state of temporary insanity. Frank Tucker, 29 years old of Ellacombe, was as much a victim of the war as those serving on the front lines and a number of suicides continued to occur in Torquay until the end of the war.

As the Aisne and Gaza battles were being fought the London battalions departed along with 1,300 men of the Royal Army Medical Corps (RAMC) who had been billeted locally. During their stay these men had spent much needed money in the local economy with the *Torquay Times* estimating that the RAMC men alone had contributed £22,000 during their stay. Their departure created some worry about how to replace this income but Torquay need not have worried. The Kiwis were coming.

Still a young nation of only a million people, New Zealand contributed greatly to the war effort with 100,000 men enlisting in the New Zealand Expeditionary Force (NZEF). Thousands of these men had been killed and many more wounded. As a result, the NZEF had chosen Torquay as the location for its discharge depot, through which unfit or discharged New Zealanders would reside while awaiting transportation home. The depot would consist of nine villas based around Torquay with the primary residences at The Daison and Hampton House in St Marychurch. Large numbers of Kiwis would now be a prominent presence in Torquay until 1919. They were exotic and far better paid than their British counterparts receiving roughly five to six times the wage of a British soldier, leading to the insult of '****in' five bobbers'. This influx of cash provided a welcome economic boost for Torquay and the town immediately became a popular destination, one soldier comparing it favourably with Wellington: 'It is lovely; it reminds me of Wellington in New Zealand, with its circular bay and terraces all round.'

On 7 May the first batch of around 100 New Zealanders arrived and three trams were requisitioned at Torre tramway station to transport the men to the Daison with the lead tram decorated with a New Zealand flag. The numbers present at the depot would vary but usually numbered between 1,500 and 1,800 men. Their impact can be understood by comparing the larger figure and Torquay's population of 38,771, this suggests that at times roughly 5.3 per cent of the residents of Torquay were New Zealanders. Given that a large percentage of the male population was no longer present, the real percentage would have been substantially higher.

While convalescing the soldiers performed a number of roles in the local economy, between 400-500 men laboured on farms at Heathfield and Lustleigh and other men were loaned to local industry. After 2pm those men not on light fatigue duty or working around the town were free to explore and socialise until 10pm. Hotels and pubs were out of bounds but this did little to prevent the more adventurous. The men soon became involved in social occasions; at a Strawberry Fete held to raise money in early July a group of Maori in full war dress performed a *haka*, probably the first time one had been performed in Torquay. The presence of the Maoris was a great talking point, most of Torquay's population had never seen a Pacific Islander before and they were fascinated in the same way American GIs would fascinate their children.

Social interaction went far beyond organised events, the ban on Kiwis visiting public houses led to locals buying them alcohol and inviting them into their houses. This was illegal but the newspapers reported it occurring almost immediately. Initially minor punishments were dealt out but as the year progressed punishments became harsher with a number of residents being imprisoned. Mary Jane Green and Kate Milton from Pimlico were sent to prison for buying drinks for New Zealanders with the *Torquay Times* suggesting less savoury things were also occurring while their husbands were away. Despite this the New Zealanders were generally well behaved, indeed such was the relationship between the townspeople and the Kiwis that it occasionally created jealousy amongst the men serving on the front. One slightly jealous Torquinian soldier wrote home asking whether 'all the gifts from Torquay go to France or to the New Zealand convalescents'.

As the New Zealanders settled into Torquay life, the BEF was once more preparing to step into the breach. The French Army was still in a mutinous state and only the BEF was able to launch an offensive. For the first time the British would take the lead in the war.

Since the beginning of the year Haig had been lobbying for an offensive in Flanders to eliminate the submarine threat and possibly turn the German flank. As the debate continued, Haig ordered Plumer to take the preliminary step: the commanding German positions on the Messines Ridge needed to be captured or they would enfilade any possible advance out of Ypres. After two years of relative obscurity, Herbert Plumer of Torquay emerged centre stage. For a war often characterised as a giant siege operation the Battle of Messines was one of the few battles explicitly planned as one. There were no grand predictions of breakthrough, the front was narrow to allow heavy artillery concentration, the advance expected of each corps was limited and once the ridge had been taken the assault would halt. After two years in which the focus had rarely been upon his front, Plumer now had his chance to shine. What was to occur was the best planned and most successful operation of the war thus far.

Plumer had realised the importance of Messines Ridge since his arrival and teams of miners had been laying mines under the ridge since mid-1915. On the eve of battle some twenty-one mines lay silently waiting for the push of a plunger. Huge quantities of artillery were moved into the area and the new techniques which had been proven at Arras were once again in use. Plumer and Rawlinson were the only British army commanders to have served in the infantry and he held a deep concern for their welfare. The infantry were heavily drilled in new tactics and a large model of the ridge was built which every officer studied in depth. Amongst those serving under Plumer were the future Field Marshal Bernard Montgomery and also the future Prime Minister Anthony Eden, who reflected:

'We were now plunged into an intensive system of training such as we had never known. Though we did not realise it at the time, subsequent events proved clearly that every aspect of training as well as the operation itself had been carefully planned by the army staff, closely supervised by Plumer, but under the direction of Harrington...It was typical that during the training of our battalion Plumer himself inspected us at work.'

This was typical of Plumer, he regularly visited troops, contrary to the myth of generals staying miles behind the frontline and he frequently ate his lunch in his motorcar between visits to the troops rather than stopping. The Reverend J.T. Jacob, now serving on the Western Front as a chaplain, reflected on the preparations:

'The effort that we expected was not to come off unrehearsed. So there were practice stunts, bursts of concentrated fire, and thousands of shells crashing into enemy positions.'

Plumer's army went into battle well trained, well organised and well supplied. Never again would the BEF be able to spend years preparing for one set piece battle and in this regard it was absolutely vital that Plumer's planning had been of the utmost quality. Unfortunately for the *Feldgrauen* patrolling the trenches atop the Messines Ridge, Herbert Plumer was about to prove himself up to the challenge. In a meeting of the press before the battle he uttered his famous quip, '*Gentlemen, we may not make history tomorrow, but we will certainly change the geography.*' He wasn't joking.

As the soldiers stood silently in their assembly trenches on the morning of 7 June, Plumer himself was reported as praying by his bedside for the men about to go into battle. At 3.10am the first of the mines exploded. The mines fired almost simultaneously apart from two which failed to ignite. Slight delays in the explosion of each mine caused the explosion to ripple down the German line as mine after mine blew the German positions skyward. Anthony Eden witnessed what was the largest intentional explosion until the advent of nuclear weapons:

'It was an astonishing sight, rising like some giant mushroom to a considerable height in the air before it suddenly broke into fragments of earth, stones and timber falling over a wide area. The whole ground heaved so violently that for a fraction of a second we thought we were over the mine instead of beside it. As the barrage opened simultaneously, the noise of the guns deadened all sound from the mine, except that we could hear, even above the crescendo, the screams of the imprisoned Germans in the crater.'

The Reverend Jacob also witnessed the explosion:

'Then, as though death and love had spoken their last words, came the roar and rumble, unlike any sound I have heard, a noise that filled one with fear of the unknown; the earth literally shuddered, this chateau trembled. This was the firing of the mines – 19 of them all at once – some of them had been prepared for nearly two years. Then the earth opened, hills became deep cups, the blue clay below came to the top…Then came the roar of artillery of all calibres – and as we put over gas shells at first, one heard a sweet musical sound running along the German lines as every gong was set going in a long gas alarm. Then the business began.'

As the mines erupted the artillery opened en masse, joining the roar of the explosions with the boom of over 2,000 guns. The artillery fired a creeping barrage ahead of the silently advancing soldiers, pounding what was left of the German trenches and neutralising the German artillery. Roughly 10,000 Germans were already dead and buried, no other non-nuclear man-made explosion has killed so many people. Writing after the event the Reverend Jacobs commented:

'There were no first line German trenches to take. They had simply been obliterated. I've been along and all you can see is a bit here and there, and there isn't shelter for a man all along the first line… It was, as a high military authority calls it, "the greatest bombardment in history" and it left light work for the infantry, too.'

Those Germans who had survived were confronted with heavily armed British soldiers charging up the ridge, curtains of shrapnel preceding them. Little resistance was initially made and forty minutes after zero hour the first objectives were taken and the initial assault wave was leapfrogged by the second wave. Resistance stiffened but the advance continued, to the south New Zealanders entered the village of Messines where a furious exchange of fire erupted between them and the Bavarians defending the town. Many New Zealanders wounded in this battle would soon find themselves being shipped back to Torquay. By around 5am the British forces stood on the crest of the ridge, beyond which they could see green fields spread out as far as the eye could see.

At 7am the barrage began to creep forward and the advance restarted, fighting was tougher as the shock of the mines wore off but the men slogged their way forward and two hours later Plumer's men were firmly established on their second objectives. At this stage casualties were surprisingly light and the German counter-attacks ran straight into the British forces achieving little. At 3.10pm the final assault down the eastern slope of the ridge began, this advance was less successful as communication and logistics were breaking down but, despite increasing casualties, these objectives were also taken.

Messines had been a resounding success, all three objectives had been taken and the

ROYAL REVIEW BY OUR SAILOR KING IN TORBAY.

ROYAL YACHT (VICTORIA & ALBERT)

H.M. KING GEORGE V.

HARBOUR & BAY TORQUAY

JULY 1910

TORBAY

(PANORAMA of BRITAINS BIGGEST ARMADA IN TORBAY)

1. The Home Fleet assembled in Torbay in 1910. Dependent upon control of the seas for her safety, Britain had engaged in an expensive naval arms race with Germany in the years leading to war and many Torquinians were serving in the navy in 1914.

2. World War One era battleship in Torbay with Paignton in the background. During the war battleships visiting the bay would have been a frequent sight. (Torquay Museum)

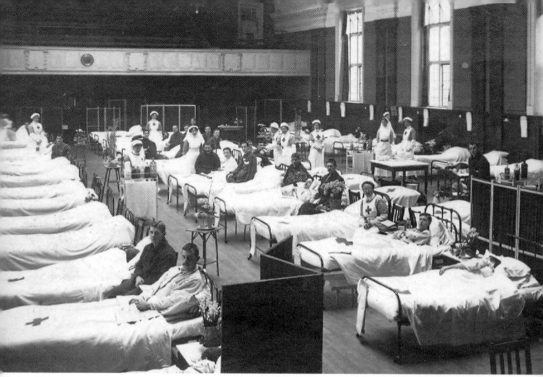

3. The Red Cross War Hospital at Torquay Town Hall, March 1915. Throughout the war thousands of British, Belgian and New Zealand soldiers would pass through Torquay hospitals. (Torquay Library)

4. A motorcade of wounded soldiers arrive from Exeter to enjoy the entertainments at the Pavilion, 22 June 1915. (Torquay Museum)

5. Torbay soldiers of the 43rd Wessex Brigade of the Territorial Force inspect an artillery gun in India. During the war many territorial soldiers would serve in India in order to free up regulars to fight on the Western Front. (Torquay Museum)

6. The Battle of Jutland 31 May – 1 June 1916: HMS *Queen Mary* explodes after gunfire from German battlecruisers *Seydlitz* and *Derfflinger*. Four Torquinians went down with the *Queen Mary* with the battle costing twenty-nine Torquinian lives, the town's worst single day of the war.

7. Infantry advancing during the Battle of the Somme, summer 1916. Although Torquay suffered relatively fewer losses on the first day than the industrial cities of Britain, the overall offensive was the bloodiest of the war for the town with at least sixty-nine Torquinians killed.

8. Rawson Ward, Torquay War Hospital. As the Battle of the Somme raged the demand on hospital beds increased and makeshift wards such as this were set up across Torquay. (Torquay Library)

9. New Zealanders resting at the Daison in 1917. During the final two years of the war they formed an increasingly prominent presence in Torquay. (Torquay Library)

10. German trenches at Messines Ridge blasted by underground mining in the opening stages of The Battle of Messines (7–14 June 1917). Planned and conducted by General Herbert Plumer it was the BEF's largest success of the war to that point. (Taylor Library)

11. 'Stand of the 2nd Devons' by William Barnes Wollen. Although only a few Torquinians were present at Bois des Buttes the battle quickly became the most celebrated of the war in the town.

12. (Opposite) Commander of the British Second Army (1915-1918) General Sir Herbert Plumer, receives a decoration from King George V. Plumer spent a substantial amount of his youth in Torquay and would later receive the freedom of the town. (Taylor Library)

13. A tank fresh from the trenches on display to the public at Daddyhole Plain, 1919. (Torquay Library)

14. The temporary war shrine assembled on the Strand following the armistice. Similar shrines were established in Hele, Cockington and St. Marychurch and formed a focal point for remembrance until the war memorial was opened. (Torquay Museum)

15. Torquay War Memorial being unveiled by Colonel Charles Burn MP, St George's Day 1921. The opening of the memorial was a conscious final action of the war for those who had served or lost loved ones during the war. (Torquay Library)

ridge was now in British hands. Alongside Arras, Messines represented a growing tactical maturity and was arguably the greatest British success of the war thus far. Compared to the Somme, casualties had been light, numbering 11,000 on the first day, German casualties were of a similar amount and more than 7,000 Germans had been captured. The BEF had ascended the learning curve sufficiently to prove it could win a set piece battle. Amongst the casualties was one Torquinian, Private William Henry Kingcome Angel of the 3rd Worcesters.

Congratulations poured in from King George V, Haig and a somewhat shocked national press. Even the Australians, notoriously prickly about British leadership, were impressed. The Official Australian History of the war stated:

'The result was a revelation – how welcome, only those who know can fully recall their own feelings at the time – that the British could plan and carry out a first class stroke with brilliant success.'

Plumer now attempted to consolidate his newly won position, a tougher job than it sounds. The Reverend Jacobs described the state of the battlefield:

'I have been over parts of the battlefield, and it has left me with what will be a perpetual nightmare. There isn't a yard of level ground; it is simply all shell craters and a line of vast mine fissures. The towns are mere heaps of builders' rubble, fallen on the cellars and underground places…I never saw such an area as the field itself. It is just not possible to describe it. It is all holes, and all over it lie torn fragments of German uniform, German accoutrements, bodies and bits of bodies, short lengths of rusty German barbed wire, all sorts of bombs, hand grenades, shells, and things that one doesn't touch…There is no blade of grass or suggestion of green.'

Running into strong resistance, Plumer urged caution but Haig used this as an excuse to transfer operations around Ypres to General Hubert Gough. In a couple months it was to fall to Gough to lead the BEF into the mud of Passchendaele.

Back on the Home Front, there still existed a firm belief that the war should continue. Colonel Burn again emphasised the need for peace on Britain's terms:

'We have got to see this war through to the very end, and then, and then only, can we lay down our terms for peace, and be able once more to resume a life more or less in accordance with our custom.'

Burn was part of the establishment and expected to support the war, however the week after Messines, a letter appeared in the *Torquay Times* from a young Torquinian officer:

'Make no doubt of one thing, we are winning slowly, and no Russian setbacks will be allowed to put the British Army out of countenance whatever happens to the people at home. But there is still an immense way to go, and I have no faith at all in any prospects of an early peace nor do I desire one, except on our terms.'

Ernest Brown also stated his support:

'The spirit of the Hun has to be wiped out in Europe, or Europe will never be free. When the boys came back they would want the old things but shame had to be wiped out and the old things infused with a new reality.'

Brown's comments are interesting because although they show a desire to continue the war, they make explicit references to the desire for change; having fought for their country many soldiers would also be expecting significant changes when they returned. As the men fought on, women continued their advance into new professions such as tramway conductors. The *Torquay Times* welcomed this development:

'Girls as tramway conductors in Torquay are a decided success. At ticket-punching and change-giving they are much smarter than the young men, and as a general rule they are pleasant and polite.

The paper's support for women conductors was a clear sign that the town was becoming increasingly comfortable with women in the workplace. Perhaps in order to ease the minds of the town's new workforce in the absence of their men, Ernest Brown made a special mention of soldiers' interactions with French women:

'The only women "Tommy" saw in France unless he was very lucky, were those who ran the farms…No man who had been out to the war and seen the sacrifice made by the average French peasant woman would ever forget the debt of gratitude we owed to France.'

His speech was economical with the truth. The idea that the average soldier barely saw a French peasant girl is debatable at best. There was substantial fraternisation between soldiers and families behind the front lines and there were officially sanctioned brothels. Despite this, by claiming that Tommy rarely saw French women, perhaps Brown made life a little more bearable for the town's women.

Since Messines, preparations had continued for the Flanders offensive but as late as mid-July Lloyd George still had not given his blessing until Admiral Jellicoe informed him that without a clearance of the Belgian ports he believed Britain would lose the war. With little alternative, Lloyd George authorised the offensive. The main objective was to capture the Passchendaele-Staden Ridge to the east of Ypres and push north to capture the ports. Although properly called the Third Battle of Ypres, it has become more commonly known as Passchendaele. Gough's plans were not the over confident plans of the Somme but they were more ambitious than Plumer's ideas, intent on reaching as far as Passchendaele on the first day. Unfortunately he had fatally decided not to focus upon the Gheluvelt Plateau to the east of Ypres, instead basing the stronger half of his army further north. Furthermore the preceding bombardment had churned up and liquidated much of the ground. Small streams such as the Steenbeek burst their banks and turned into morasses of mud. It was not ground across which to launch a major offensive.

On 31 July the Battle of Passchendaele began and at first all went well. Protected by a creeping barrage, Gough's men were soon deep into the German front line until the counter-attacks hit. The ambitious objectives set by Gough left the advancing infantry exhausted and out of artillery support in contrast to the staggered leaps of Messines. Most of the early gains were lost as the British were flung staggering back. In the early afternoon the first drops of drizzly rain began to fall and soon it began to pour as the attack failed in the face of the mud and the artillery on the Gheluvelt Plateau. There were 31,000 casualties in the first three days in exchange for a similar number of German casualties, and two Torquinian soldiers fell, Corporal James Frederick Bourhill and Corporal Roy Alexander McMorran.

Throughout August Gough's men continued to attack as the battleground turned into a filthy morass of liquid mud, barbed wire and human bodies. Both sides clashed in and around water-filled shell craters so deep that a man could drown. Throughout these attacks the rain fell mercilessly; soldiers who slipped off the duckboards leading the way through the battlefield, were likely to die in the rain filled craters. The worse the British position became, the more Gough persisted.

In amongst the carnage, Norman Cliff returned to active service, fully recovered from his wound:

'Within a few days it was up to the line again and everything conspired to make me feel completely at home. Rain poured upon us as we made our way, providing the familiar mud, and there was Ypres as stark a ruin as ever.'

Gough protested that success in such conditions was impossible but Haig stressed the need to continue. Turning to Plumer, he asked him to create a diversion but Plumer had no intention of wasting lives and refused. On 25 August Haig's patience snapped and he handed control of the battle to Plumer, tasking him with the capture of the Gheluvelt Plateau that had so conspicuously failed to be secured. Plumer agreed on the proviso that he had three weeks to prepare.

As the soldiers slogged through the mud, attention at home once more turned to the anniversary of the war. The *Torquay Times* reflected:

'Events have occurred which have made us realize that Torquay is not so far away from the war zone, as was thought to be the case in the early days. Dead and wounded seamen have been landed at our harbour, and we have heard the guns booming almost close at hand. Very few young men have been left in our midst, and there has been an increase of pressure on the business life of the Borough.'

Figures published in the *Directory* revealed that since the start of the war 253,405 soldiers of British and Belgian descent had passed through the town's war hospitals. Elsewhere there were continued worries about the local food supply. Colonel Burn wrote urging the population to save food:

'Will you sir, tell my constituents that in the year before the war far more fresh food was left in dustbins than all the German submarines have destroyed during 1916 and 1917 put together…Much still remains to be done if we are to wear out our determined adversaries by attrition…We can, if we so resolve, out-last the Germans.'

War profiteering was also becoming noticeable. In mid-July potatoes cost 1d per lb in Teignmouth but in Torquay the price was double. This rise in costs hit the poor the hardest and in mid-June a communal kitchen was opened, and in August a committee for food control established. Not only were prices increasing but availability was decreasing at a fast rate. National consumption of butter in October was nearly half the level of the previous year, with bacon suffering a similar decline. Despite these economic struggles, there were some who were looking to the future, the *Torquay Times* suggesting that after the war a great trade between Britain and France could occur through Torquay as France rebuilt herself.

As Gough floundered in the mud, Plumer was preparing. He had not forgotten the lessons of Messines and his battles would be fought on narrow fronts with overwhelming artillery support and employing staggered leaps. These tactics were designed to wear down the opponent, not to decisively breakthrough and were far more suited to the battle than Gough's ambitions. Furthermore the rains had now ceased and Plumer had dry weather to bring his supplies and artillery forward. On 20 September he launched his first hammer blow in the Battle of the Menin Road Ridge. Aided by the weather and the kind of thorough preparation that was his trademark, nearly all the objectives were taken. Ludendorff summed up the battle:

'The enemy's onslaught on the 20th was successful, which proved the superiority of the attack over the defence. Its strength did not consist in the tanks; we found them inconvenient, but put them out of action all the same. The power of the attack lay in the artillery.'

Despite the success of the battle, casualties were still heavy, numbering around 20,000 including a single Torquinian, Second Lieutenant William Louis Bridgman. From a strictly military sense they were sustainable on the British side but not on the German. Germany's manpower was running low and she could not succeed in a war of attrition.

Plumer immediately began preparations for the next leap forward which took place on 26 September with the Battle of Polygon Wood. In an attempt to maintain surprise the preliminary bombardment lasted only a day. The result was the same as before. The success of Menin Road and Polygon Wood led to the German commanders switching from thinly held front lines to a heavily held front line in an attempt to blunt the initial British attack. This wasn't to have much success.

On 4 October Plumer launched his third blow against the creaking German edifice, the Battle of Broodseinde. The preliminary artillery barrage was almost entirely excluded and the artillery did not open until the infantry were advancing. Once again the Germans were swept aside. Although casualties were once again heavy, the battle being the equal bloodiest day for Torquay in 1917 with eight Torquinians killed, Plumer considered the victory even greater than Messines. Ludendorff, despairing of the relentless advance stated:

'Once again we only came through it with enormous losses. It was evident that the idea of holding the front line more densely...was not the remedy.'

The Reverend Jacobs wrote home describing the falling morale of German soldiers facing the onslaught:

'They were all fine men, but absolutely done for, their nerves were all gone...Their field grey uniform was caked with mud, and they were unshaven, shaky and miserable looking men. One of them said to me "It is better here, it is awful there".'

Since Plumer had taken command the BEF had advanced relentlessly, his men had proved they could break into any position and hold it against counter-attacks. It seemed only a matter of time until a decisive breakthrough was made. Although British casualties were high, they were not exceptional, the Germans on the other hand were losing men at an unsustainable rate. Then the skies opened once more. Torrential rain fell and the logistics of the BEF crumbled.

Haig was determined to continue but, despite being against the idea Plumer and Gough, confirmed they would if asked. Plumer should have been more forceful with his objections but was perhaps becoming over-confident. The continuation of the offensive was his biggest mistake of the war. The weather had broken and it was impossible to transport artillery to the front line. Reginald Colwill, a Torquinian present painted a vivid picture of the battlefield:

'Look for a moment at a pan of fat, gently simmering on the fire. See how little bubbles work up and burst, one across the other, covering the surface of the fat with little pits. Imagine this to be magnified several million times, and fancy the pits big enough to bury a horse and cart in – at the smallest – and some of them large enough to entomb a house. Think of these pits as being in the earth, brimful of water and slimy mud; think of it stretching for mile after mile, as far as the eye will reach, and then you may catch some faint glimpse of what the district was like between Ypres and Passchendaele.'

The careful preparation that had been Plumer's *modus operandi* was also conspicuously lacking as the preparation time between each assault was shortened in an exaggeration of the first three battles. It was against this backdrop that Plumer launched the last actions of Passchendaele. On 9 October the Battle of Poelcappelle was fought, gaining little ground as the battlefield had been churned into a bog and artillery was almost impossible to move forward. A further two Torquinians were killed as Plumer's men struggled in the mire. On the far left of the front the Guards Division supported Plumer's advance, Norman Cliff describing the scene:

'The approach to the ridge was a desolate swamp, over which brooded an evil menacing atmosphere that seemed to defy encroachment. Far more treacherous than the visible surface defences with which we were familiar, such as barbed wire, deep devouring mud spread deadly traps in all directions. We splashed and slithered, and dragged our feet from the pull of an invisible enemy determined to suck us into its depths. Every few steps someone would slide and stumble and weighed down by rifle and equipment, rapidly sink into the squelching mess. Those nearest grabbed his arms, struggled against being themselves engulfed and, if humanly possible, dragged him out. When helpers floundered in as well and doubled the task, it became hopeless. All the straining efforts failed, the swamp swallowed its screaming victims, and we had to be ordered to plod on dejectedly and fight this relentless enemy as stubbornly as we did those we could see....To be ordered to go ahead and leave a comrade to such a fate was the hardest experience one could be asked to endure, but the objective had to be reached, and we plunged on, bitter anger against the evil forces prevailing piled on to our exasperation. This was as near to Hell as I ever want to be.'

On 12 October, the First Battle of Passchendaele also failed, the artillery barrage once again being inadequate. The situation was now desperate, men were fighting waist deep in water in parts, it was impossible to bring supplies forward and men lay slowly dying for days if they hadn't already drowned in the flooded shell holes. As a result of the destruction of his papers we'll never know why Plumer launched these final battles. Perhaps he had become over-confident and believed that a breakthrough was within his grasp. Regardless, the decision to continue was a huge mistake and Haig, Plumer and Gough finally agreed that no further advance should be attempted until the weather improved.

As the month progressed the weather became better and, with the ability to bring supplies and artillery forward, thorough preparations were undertaken in line with the earlier trilogy of victories. On 26 October the Canadians, who had refused to serve under Gough, spearheaded the Second Battle of Passchendaele and by 6 November they had finally secured their objective. On the opening day of this battle, eight Torquinians fell, equalling Broodseinde as the bloodiest day of the year without the same feeling of success.

Politics intervened and Plumer was denied being present to see Passchendaele captured. The Italians had been smashed in the Battle of Caporetto and Lloyd George had leapt upon this opportunity to send British reinforcements. Highly regarded after his year's work, even after his recent failures, Plumer was given command of the army being sent to Italy. He did not want to go; in a letter to his wife he claimed:

'I have just received a great shock. I have been ordered to go to Italy to assume command of the British forces there. I am very sick about it and do not want to go in the least.'

In Plumer's mind his place was in Flanders with his men but he had no choice. Shortly thereafter Haig finally ended the offensive. With the exception of August, Plumer had been in command from Messines until Second Passchendaele. During this period he had proved to be an astute and well prepared commander, valuing the importance of limited objectives, heavy artillery bombardments and well trained infantry. He secured impressive victories at Messines, Menin Road Ridge, Polygon Wood and Broodseinde but Poelcappelle and First Passchendaele were also his biggest mistakes of the war. Despite this he was one of the best British generals of the war.

The Third Ypres campaign was the second most costly offensive of the war for Torquay with at least 57 local men killed. Despite the huge number of casualties it was arguably a strategic British victory, the ports remained in German hands but the offensive had inflicted huge losses upon the Germans that were becoming increasingly hard to replace and the French Army had been given time to recover from its problems. The realisation that these losses were becoming unsustainable would play a key role in Germany's gamble in the coming spring.

The casualties suffered since 1914 left many people struggling to come to terms with how to commemorate their loved ones. It had been decided that all fallen soldiers would be buried where they fell, as many poor families could not afford to repatriate their loved ones and it was considered politically unwise to allow the rich to do so. As a result, throughout the summer war shrines began to appear in Torquay listing the fallen. The first mention of a shrine was in Hele during August, swiftly followed by Torre and then Cockington. These shrines became immensely popular and spiritualism was becoming more pronounced as people took to believing they could contact the dead despite the churches' condemnation. Percy Fawcett was a prominent local example as he began exchanging letters with Arthur Conan Doyle discussing mediums.

The final British offensive of the year occurred at Cambrai on 20 November. Impressive gains were made when forces, including 437 tanks, broke into the supposedly impregnable Hindenburg Line and made advances of three to four miles. It was the first large scale use of tanks but the primary reason for success was the surprise bombardment adopted by the artillery. Previously they had been required to range their guns by firing test bombardments, this lengthy process gave away the fact an attack was imminent. Now further advances provided the ability to open a bombardment without having to range guns. This delivered a huge shock to the defending Germans but success was fleeting and counter-attacks regained large swathes of the newly won ground. Although it failed to capture Cambrai, the battle once again proved that given sufficient preparation the BEF could break into any sector of the German front. Furthermore the mass use of tanks showed how the army was groping its way towards a combined arms doctrine.

Losses were relatively small totalling seven from Torquay. Thus the year ended much as it had begun. The offensives at Arras, Messines, Passchendaele and Cambrai cost hundreds of thousands of casualties however the BEF had continued to advance along the learning curve, now firmly grasping the concept of limited objective battles. Aircraft and tanks were being used in ever greater amounts. If it could combine the individual victories it was achieving into a string of victories, the war may yet be won.

Over Christmas peace was being spoken about more openly and in Torquay portraits of Woodrow Wilson began to be displayed prominently. News also filtered through of the capture of Jerusalem, to such a religious people the news would have been greeted with joy but it was small consolation for the year's efforts. Torquay had suffered 190 men killed, the highest total of the entire war. The average age of fallen soldiers was also decreasing, from 28.11 years old in 1916 to 27.33 years old, showing the increasing reliance on young conscripted men. At times during Passchendaele and Cambrai breakthrough had fleetingly beckoned but had then been cruelly snatched away. Britain and Torquay had endured their worst year of the war but Germany had failed to break their will. Little did anyone realise how close the war was to its conclusion.

However to reach the endgame, the BEF would have to weather the thunderstorm slowly building across the Western Front. Its name was the *Kaiserschlacht*.

Chapter 5

1918 – Endgame

*'Only fools and those who have never seen war will talk of "the glories of war".
There are no glories of war, in the ordinarily accepted meaning of the word...but there
is glory in devotion and sacrifice that others may benefit.'*
Reginald A. Colwill, Torquinian present at Bois des Buttes

The year 1918 began with more privations on the Home Front, the Reverend Jacobs
urging his townspeople to stick it out in the name of solidarity:

'Before you lies the path of real sacrifice, of discipline in food, of a more rigid
economy...Those abroad will never let those at home down, cost it even life itself.
Let those at home be just as heroic and ready to sacrifice as those abroad. If the
two armies, that at home and that abroad, pull together, there is absolutely no
doubt as to the result. We have to hold on to the bitter end.'

Anger bubbled up to the surface and a spat broke out between Torquay and Brixham
when insinuations were made that people were buying cream without the correct
documentation in Brixham. This soon drew an angry response:

'Is there no one in Torquay who has purchased cream without a certificate?
Methinks that our neighbouring "delightful summer resort" is just a little jealous
that this little fishing port has in the past been extra fortunate in their supplies.
Another honourable member suggests the Utopian ideal of "meat without bone"
which we fortunate folk of Brixham enjoy. Oh! That it were true. Let the
gentleman come here with his coupons and purchase his next Sunday's joint!'

Despite the belt tightening Torquay was still contributing to the war effort; the
government had proposed that the town raise £100,000 for a submarine and, taking
enthusiastically to the cause, Torquay raised £127,536 by mid-March, shattering the
amount expected. Manuel II of Portugal and his wife were once again in town and the
former Australian Prime Minister Andrew Fisher also arrived for a short break.

One Torquinian holidaying elsewhere was Pierre Brottin, who wrote to say that he'd
been temporarily discharged due to severe wounds and was residing at Eastbourne.
Having served since 1914 it was a deserved rest.

Elsewhere, despite being banned from the town's public houses, the New Zealanders
were making the most of their high wages. The *Directory* rather blatantly reprinted a
letter from *The Times* warning families to be wary of overseas troops proposing to their
daughters. These warnings did little to put off the locals, there were reports of women
being absent from war work and of many marriage proposals. In a sign of how fully
Torquay had taken these men to her heart a detachment of soldiers left the town for New
Zealand taking with them 150 women they had married during their stay.

The other major event of that winter was women finally being given the vote. Lady Acland, who had so eloquently urged Torquay's women to get behind the war effort in 1914, stated:

'It is perhaps hard for men who have always possessed the franchise to realise the relief which many women will now feel, that in future their opinions, remonstrances and advice will carry equal weight with those of male voters. The sense that "I am only a vote-less woman, and cannot expect any attention from members of parliament" has been at the bottom of much bitterness.'

Torquay, despite having an unusually large percentage of women, had never been a hotbed of suffragettes but nevertheless the news was met with much satisfaction.

Following Passchendaele, Lloyd-George was no longer content to acquiesce to the BEF's demands. Haig requested 615,000 men as reinforcements but Lloyd-George refused, providing only 200,000 while forcing Haig to take control of a new sector of the front from St Quentin to the Oise River. The positions forced upon the BEF were in an extremely poor state and the dearth of reinforcements meant that it lacked the manpower needed to repair them. The BEF would now have to hold more of the line than ever with fewer soldiers than previously.

As Haig and Lloyd-George argued, the Prime Minister openly considered replacing his adversary, with Plumer being among the favourites, but ultimately decided to leave Haig in position. Having spent the winter reorganising the Italian Front, Plumer received the call to return to Ypres, he boarded a train back to France, little realising what he would return to.

The *Kaiserschlacht*, Germany's Spring Offensive was the last throw of the dice, a grand plan designed to win the war before the Americans could deploy in force or the German home front collapsed. With over a million reinforcements arriving following Russia's withdrawal from the war, Ludendorff planned a series of huge offensives with the intention of knocking the British out of the war before defeating the French. Operation Michael, the first of the *Kaiserschlacht* offensives, began at 4.40am on 21 March near the old battlefields of the Somme. Seventy-six German divisions attacked against just twenty-six under-strength British. The Reverend Jacobs wrote of the opening bombardment:

'The bombardment started at 4am...They poured in gas and made a terrific barrage. In one place they had eight divisions in the space usually occupied by two divisions, and have evidently been hoping they would smash the British by sheer weight of numbers'.

German stormtroopers infiltrated the devastated British positions as a heavy fog lingered, many slipping past the defenders and into the rear before the British even realised the offensive had begun. Regular soldiers followed in their wake and chaos erupted across the front. No communications could get through, battalions were surrounded and attacked from all sides with no hope of escape. By early afternoon Gough's Fifth Army had been forced to order a fighting retreat, forcing the right of Byng's Third Army to follow. The German advance reached eight miles deep in some sectors, more than the entire advance at the Somme or Passchendaele. Two British armies were in retreat and threatening to open a dangerous gap between themselves and the French and, for the first time since 1914, open warfare resumed. During the chaos Torquay suffered six deaths. Fighting over the following two days descended into localised actions as the hard pressed British soldiers were forced back across the old Somme battlefields. Soldiers staggered in confusion through the winding streets of Albert where they were bombed and strafed by German aircraft and many wounded men had to be left where they fell:

'[I was] smothered in dust and soaked in blood from lifting wounded into the only ambulance available – ignoring a doctor who at first refused to take those who were obviously on the way out...I shall never forget the appealing look in the eyes of one of our sappers who was refused. I always look for his name on the war memorial on Torquay seafront when I am there.'

As Gough and Byng's armies fell back, Ludendorff drove his armies towards the vital railway hub of Amiens. This was a critical change from his initial plan of cutting off the BEF and pushing it northwards. By 24 March the Somme had been lost and the Reverend Jacobs wrote home about the seriousness of the situation:

'I verily believe that even now there are people in England, perhaps even in fair Torquay that corner of paradise so far removed from the horrors of the war, who are not yet irate with Germany, the foul traitor to the human race, to God, to pity and honour, but who are only cross because the war causes them inconvenience. I wish such people could be brought here, and stand face to face with the heroic, unselfish, brave French...We must, and I hope the people in England will say, we shall fight to a finish. Better death than the nightmare of existence under the Kaiser.'

Surprisingly the advance now began slowing, heavy casualties had been suffered, the advance over the devastated Somme was causing huge logistical problems and serious issues with discipline were emerging. Coming across Allied supply dumps after months of privation the German soldiers began looting and getting drunk.

On the Allied side Ferdinand Foch had been made Supreme Commander of the Allied armies and had fully committed the French Army to the defence of Amiens after fears the French would retreat upon Paris. On 28 March, Ludendorff switched focus to hammer the Third Army around Arras, this poorly prepared attack was a total failure, the same day Gough was sacked and replaced by Henry Rawlinson. Despite his poor leadership at Passchendaele, Gough had performed heroics throughout March but someone had to carry the blame for the immense losses suffered. The German armies had advanced a huge distance but on the front held by Byng's Third Army, where Ludendorff needed to breakthrough to isolate the BEF, results had been less impressive. The improving situation amongst the BEF was reflected in an over optimistic but revealing letter from a Torquinian officer:

'the spirit of the men is wonderful. They are as bright and cheerful as ever, despite the fact they are going through absolute hell; it is far and away the worst phase of the war up to the present, but there is no need to get the wind up. One thing which did strike me was the arrival of thousands of young recruits, lots of them from Devon. I came across boys from Exeter, Plymouth, Newton, Torquay and one from Churston Ferrers, which was very interesting. The sight of these youngsters alone ought to make those who are fit and of military age fly to the colours. I can assure you that every man who is fit will be needed to make the issue successful…As far as Amiens is concerned, I don't think for a moment that the Germans will ever take it.'

On 30 March and 4 April the weakened German armies lunged towards Amiens but few gains were made and Operation Michael finally ran out of steam. Haig had been left with just one division in reserve. The BEF had survived the first thrust of the *Kaiserschlacht* but it had been a close run thing and Torquay had suffered sixteen casualties. Operation Michael surprisingly harmed the Germans to a greater extent than the British.

Lloyd-George, who had contributed greatly to the BEF's struggles, began releasing reinforcements immediately and combined with the arriving Americans the losses suffered would soon be replaced while the Germans had suffered 239,000 casualties which they could barely replace. The advance had reached 40 miles deep in places but Amiens and Arras remained under British control and much of the ground now under German control was useless. Having failed to win the war on the Somme, Ludendorff's attention now turned to Plumer's Second Army, standing sentinel on the ridges above Ypres.

On 1 April amongst the confusion of the *Kaiserschlacht*, the RAF was officially created, followed by the establishment of RAF Torquay. The Torquay base, Number 239 Squadron, was based on Beacon Quay and consisted of twelve seaplanes and a number of observation balloons to combat the submarine threat. Six American submarine chasers also arrived in Torquay to undergo training.

At the height of Operation Michael, Plumer had been forced to release his best divisions southwards and in return had received the shattered remnants of those caught up in the fighting and new drafts of raw 19-year-olds. This new Second Army was far from the battle hardened formation of the previous year and Plumer would now face the brunt of the second *Kaiserschlacht* offensive, codenamed Operation Georgette by the Germans and for the Allies the Battle of the Lys.

It began on 9 April smashing into General Horne's First Army to the south of Plumer. The Germans had the good fortune of hitting an exhausted Portuguese division and by the end of the day an advance of six miles had been made. The following day they threatened to break through to the railway centre of Hazebrouck and recaptured Messines, throwing Plumer's men back to the outskirts of Wytschaete. In an attempt to encourage his men Plumer was regularly on the front lines visiting his divisions and encouraging them but the Germans were steadily grinding their way towards Ypres. Haig now issued his famous 'Backs against the Wall' speech making clear what was at risk:

'Many amongst us are now tired. To those I would say that victory will belong to the side which holds out the longest. The French Army is moving rapidly and in great force to our support. There is no other course available to us but to fight it out. Every position must be held to the last man; there must be no retirement. With our backs to the wall and believing in the justice of our cause each one of us must fight on to the end. The safety of our homes and the freedom of mankind alike depend upon the conduct of each one of us at this critical moment.'

With Messines in German hands, the British hold on the Passchendaele Ridge became precarious. In desperate need to shorten his front line Plumer considered the unthinkable, to relinquish the ridge that so many lives had been given to capture; his anguish must have been immense. On 14 April he made his decision, when his chief of staff Harrington pressed upon Plumer the need to retreat, he refused and walked out of the room before returning and placing his hands on Harrington's shoulder stated, 'You are right. Issue the orders'. The withdrawal was conducted flawlessly but the BEF had now lost all the gains of 1917 and the front line was once more at the gates of Ypres. Here the BEF would stand or fall.

Three days later the Germans switched focus, launching themselves at the range of hills that spread westward from Messines in an attempt to encircle Ypres, battles ground on for days but Operation Georgette spluttered to a halt. Plumer's motley army had survived and when the dust settled Georgette had made fewer gains than Michael. By the end of these operations the BEF had suffered 236,300 casualties, including 24 Torquinians, and been pushed to the limit of its endurance; but a further 270,000 British soldiers had arrived on the Western Front alongside six new American divisions. The clock was ticking.

At the same time as Georgette was raging, the navy launched a raid against Zeebrugge and Ostend in an attempt to put their submarine bases out of action, it had mixed success with two blockships being successfully sunk in the mouth of the Zeebrugge-Bruges Canal but the marines involved in the operation had encountered heavy resistance. Amongst them was Lieutenant Commander Arthur Leyland Harrison, English Rugby Union international from Torquay. Harrison died while leading a detachment of marines at Zeebrugge. In the words of the *London Gazette*:

'The silencing of the guns on the Mole head was of the first importance, and though in a position fully exposed to the enemy's machine-gun fire Lieut.-Commander Harrison gathered his men together and led them to the attack. He was killed at the head of his men, all of whom were either killed or wounded.'

As Harrison fell to the ground dead, Captain Edward Bamford, another Torquinian, attempted to salvage something from the chaos:

'When on the mole and under fire he displayed the greatest initiative in the command of his company, and by his total disregard of danger, showed a magnificent example to his men. He first established a strongpoint on the right of the disembarkation, and, when satisfied that that was safe, led an assault on a battery to the left with the utmost coolness and valour.'

For their efforts both Harrison and Bamford were awarded the Victoria Cross. It was the first time a Torquinian had won the Victoria Cross in the war and it elicited great pride. Unfortunately submarines were operating from Zeebrugge again within months but for Torquay the raid will always be associated with Harrison and Bamford.

Attention now turned back to land where Ludendorff was preparing another sledgehammer blow with Operation Blücher-Yorck. Unlike previous operations it would hit the French but six battle-ravaged British divisions lay in the line of advance. These exhausted divisions would meet the full fury of the offensive and in doing so one battalion of the Devons would write its name into history.

Following Operation Michael, the 2nd Devons had moved to the Chemin des Dames to recuperate. Initially they had a quiet time but by 26 May the peaceful relaxation was over and they were ordered to prepare for battle. At the headquarters of their brigade on the night before the offensive, Captain Phillip Ledward reflected on what was to come:

'There was an ominous silence of the German guns all night, but ours kept banging away. Grogan made the pretence of going to bed, but I sat up reading Blackwood's magazine, with my watch on the table in front of me. It was a hot still night and the feeling of suspense and tension was, speaking for myself, very acute. I haven't now the faintest notion of what I was reading.'

That evening the 2nd Devons received their orders to form the brigade reserve in the Bois des Buttes, occupying trenches on two hills within the woods and sheltering in tunnels that cut through them. At 12.45am on 27 May, Lieutenant Colonel Rupert Anderson-Morshead, commanding officer, held a conference with his company commanders, explaining that an attack was to occur at 1am and reminding them of the French instructions that not a foot of ground was to be given up, the men then shared a bottle of whisky. 'How quiet it all is,' observed one officer. Anderson-Morshead looked at his watch. The time had come and sure enough two dull thuds were heard. Gas shells. Then the German artillery erupted. Captain Sydney Rogerson, at brigade headquarters, described the bombardment:

'A thousand guns roared out their iron hurricane. The night was rent with sheets of flame. The earth shuddered under the avalanche of missiles, leapt skywards in dust and tumult. Even above the din screamed the fierce crescendo of approaching shells, ear-splitting crashes as they burst. All the time the dull thud, thud, thud of detonations and drum fire. Inferno raged and whirled around the Bois des Buttes….It was a descent into hell.'

Two million shells were fired in little more than four hours. Throughout the early morning the Devons remained underground, sheltering as loose soil fell from above. Gas masks were hurriedly pulled on as gas seeped into their underground refuge through every available crack. What the soldiers huddling together in the cramped tunnels were thinking can only be guessed. Some of the more sarcastic old timers told the youngsters that they would all be 'blown to bits before breakfast'. At 3.40am the first stormtroopers began to advance and hit the West Yorks and Middlesex men in the front line trenches. The Devons were now on their own.

Shortly thereafter they exited their shelters and took position in the trenches throughout the woods. Most had been pounded flat and telephone communications to the rear were severed. Three companies assembled at the front of the hill, B on the left, D in the centre and C to the right, Anderson-Morshead and A Company remained at the rear. Artillery fire was raining down around them and from his position Anderson-Morshead could not see the full disposition of his companies nor the oncoming Germans in the mist. All attempts to make contact ended in failure. Ahead of him the Germans had already advanced deep into the battle zone trenches. This was repeated across the battlefield, General Duchêne had rejected the idea of defence in depth and as a result large numbers of troops were being overrun. To the left of B Company, 50th Division troops were already falling back leaving B Company's left flank dangerously in the air. As the Devons emerged, many found stormtroopers already in their trenches. B Company was the first to be hit, an eye witness describing the Devons during this period as 'merely an island in the midst of an innumerable and determined foe'. Private A.J. Bourne gives a good view of the initial fighting:

> 'I was with the Lewis gun team, and we were first in action. All my pals of the team were speedy casualties, including Gennoe and Roberts. Lads were falling right and left, but I had a capital weapon in the Lewis gun, which I was firing steadily at the German hordes. I looked about, and I seemed to be all alone. Still, I kept firing at them.'

Casualties were high and B Company was quickly surrounded, their spirited defence being extinguished by sheer numbers. As they were being destroyed, the Germans advanced around the left flank of the Bois des Buttes to cut off the Devons' retreat. D Company was heavily engaged from the front and C Company was being assaulted from the front and right as the enemy also attempted to advance around the right flank. Artillery pounded their positions, machine guns raked them from the front and aircraft strafed them from above. At this point the remnants of the Middlesex and West Yorks soldiers began flooding through the Devons, Captain Ulick Burke describes the scene:

> 'We had lots of Middlesex wounded coming back through us. They got over the river, back over the Pontavert Bridge behind us. Then the West Yorks who were in support started coming back and they went through us. The order was to stay put as long as we could – we were not to retire! We stayed where we were. We shot and shot and shot till the fellows in the trenches could hardly hold their rifles.'

Lieutenant Tindall of C Company also noticed the retreating men and engaged in a conversation with his officers about whether they should hold position. It was decided to hold to the last and noticing the German flanking attempt, what was left of C Company attacked. One soldier present described the assault:

> 'Lieut. Tindall ordered us to fix bayonets and get ready to charge. We now saw the enemy in tremendous force, and it seemed, from the very start, to be a hopeless thing to charge them. But we had been put there to check the advance, and this appeared the only way to do it. They were almost on us before we had a chance to use the rifle to any extent, but we managed to inflict terrible damage on them. We had one Lewis gun and until it was put out of action with a hand grenade, L/Corpl. Hannaford [a Torquinian] used it to good purpose'.

As C Company battled to prevent the German flanking attempt Tindall was shot through the head and fell to the ground. C Company fought their desperate stand and D Company in the centre was engaged in an equally epic battle. They traded trenches with the Germans three times, each time repulsing the enemy with bayonets. Lieutenant F.E. Harris at one point noticed a German aircraft flying low over the battle and leapt onto a trench and called upon his men to shoot at it. The pilot noticing this brash act opened fire upon him, slightly grazing his arm, at which he exclaimed: 'I believe the beggar did it on purpose!'

Another officer amongst D Company, Lieutenant C.E. Pells, fought with almost inhuman ferocity against the oncoming soldiers; his only child had died onboard the *Lusitania*. C and D companies fought like mad men but had taken exceptionally heavy casualties. As the officers fell, the NCOs took charge and when they fell leadership passed to recruits of eighteen and nineteen. Step by step they were forced back and the companies began to fragment into isolated groups of men fighting desperately to their end. On both flanks the Germans were now encircling those who remained, the few who escaped fell back on what remained of A Company.

At 8.30am, Anderson-Morshead gathered together the shattered remnants and retreated to the rear of the Bois des Buttes. They were now being assaulted from three directions. He split his men into three groups, each covering one route of advance and grimly awaited the inevitable, telling his men: 'Your job for England, men, is to hold the blighters up as much as you can…There is no hope of relief. We have to fight to the last.' These remnants fought to their last, many falling in vicious hand-to-hand combat and at 9.30am Anderson-Morshead and his last fifty men charged off the rear of the hill to assault a German artillery detachment where he was shot and killed.

Captain Burke now took command. Despite having nine machine gun bullets in his legs and being incapacitated, he prepared his men to fight their final action:

'As far as we were concerned there were just twenty-three of us, we had just about 200 rounds of ammunition left…We went on firing until all the ammunition was gone. We held on 'til about half past twelve when the only ammunition left was six rounds in my revolver. Suddenly, I said "Charge!"…Twenty-three men charged against nearly 10,000 Germans. That finished us".'

With that last valiant charge the Battle of Bois des Buttes was over and 551 (23 officers and 528 men) of the Devons who had started the battle were posted as killed or missing. The battalion had been destroyed. With their sacrifice they bought vital time and 8th Division's commander credited their actions with allowing the Allied forces across the Aisne to regroup into some kind of ad hoc defence.

At least three Torquinians were present at Bois des Buttes, Sergeant C.S. Hooper, the previously mentioned Fred Hannaford and Reginald Colwill. Months later reports stated that Hooper was now a prisoner of war perhaps captured during the battle. Bois des Buttes ranks alongside the greatest actions by a British battalion during the war. The Devons had stood and fought to the end and their sacrifice would not be forgotten.

With the Devons defeated the Germans crossed the Aisne, by 30 May they were on the Marne for the first time since 1914 and on 3 June Paris was shelled with a million citizens fleeing. However Operation Blücher-Yorck ultimately failed to capture Paris as did Operation Gneisnau in the middle of June. The German Army outran its logistics and was once again subject to a breakdown in discipline. Allied counter-attacks stiffened and the Americans finally joined the fray. On 15 July Ludendorff launched his last great offensive, the *Freidenssturm* (Peace Offensive), three days later the French counter-attacked using over 300 tanks and forced the Germans to retreat from all their gains since Blücher-Yorck. The *Kaiserschlacht* was over.

Since 21 March nearly four months had passed, throughout those months a German victory had seemed only a matter of weeks away but through it all the Allies had endured. Torquay lost 49 men during the *Kaiserschlacht*, the worst offensive of the war other than the Somme and Passchendaele. For Germany the failure sowed the seeds of her defeat. German soldiers had been shocked by the abundant supplies they found which increased the ongoing decline in their morale. Furthermore she had exhausted the last of her manpower reserves and was no closer to victory. The Americans were now joining battle in ever increasing numbers and they were joined by British soldiers returning from distant fronts. Far from breaking the Allies, after the *Kaiserschlacht* they emerged stronger than before. The war's final act would soon be played out.

Meanwhile Torquay attempted to continue as best it could. The presence of large numbers of New Zealanders meant that the new celebration of 'ANZAC Day' was celebrated with much gusto, the High Commissioner sharing in the celebrations, but everyday life on the home front was increasingly tough and rationing was extended to butter, margarine, lard, meat and sugar. The German offensives had caused yet another influx of wounded soldiers to the town's hospitals and Torquay Town Hall was now the largest war hospital in Devon with 238 beds, the nearest rival being Plymouth with 185. The *Kaiserschlacht* had also captured many British soldiers and at least 35 Torquinians were now prisoners of war. Suspicious of the treatment their men were receiving, the town once more mobilised its finances in an effort to raise money to buy items to send to Germany for them.

A surprising number of local men were still serving in the army at this late stage of the war. With a general election scheduled, a census of absent men was held to ensure they received their vote. Some of these censuses still exist, unfortunately not Torquay's but references in the media give an insight to the number of men still fighting.

AREA OF TORQUAY	NUMBER OF SOLDIERS SERVING
Babbacombe	447
Ellacombe South	752
Ellacombe North	217
St. Marychurch	498
Strand	338
Torre	329
Torwood	223
Upton South	328
Upton North	327
Waldon	325
Chelston (Not part of Torquay in 1918)	254
Cockington (Not Part of Torquay in 1918)	23
Torquay Total (exc. Chelston/Cockington)	3,784

Torquay Soldiers Serving in mid-1918 according to the Absent Voters List
Source: Torbay News, August 21, 1918

Torquay was providing nearly four battalions worth of soldiers, meaning that even during this late period, 22.21 per cent of the male population was serving. The figure for the whole Torquay Parliamentary Division, which also covered Paignton, Brixham, Dartmouth and Kingswear, was 7,827 men, close to a division. In mid-August the manager of the Imperial Hotel offered £100 towards a memorial for fallen Torquinians. This was a natural progression from the war shrine movement and the first public suggestion of a civic memorial, but there was still a war to be won.

As summer reached its peak, the BEF was ready to return to the offensive. Foch, in concert with Haig, had developed an ambitious plan of hitting the weakened Germans on a number of fronts in quick succession and the first action was to be fought where Operation Michael had faltered. The Battle of Amiens announced the beginning of the end for Germany. As at Cambrai there would be no preliminary bombardment and the battle was planned as a large-scale tank assault designed to punch a hole in the German lines for the infantry to exploit. The entire Tank Corps of 552 vehicles was to be deployed including new Mark Vs and Whippet tanks capable of eight miles per hour.

The infantry were also better prepared than they had ever been, despite their falling numbers, numbering roughly 50,000 compared to 100,000 on the Somme. Each battalion now carried thirty machine guns compared to four in 1916, eight trench mortars compared to one or two, and sixteen grenade-throwing rifles. This increase in firepower was combined with the leapfrogging tactics perfected in the previous year and tactics were now organised at platoon level allowing a great degree of flexibility. The RAF also innovated by air dropping ammunition and smoke bombs. Prior to the battle they performed a key role in spotting many of the German artillery positions. This combination of infantry, artillery, tanks and aircraft hinted at the future of war.

At 4.20am on 8 August the artillery opened fire at the same time as the infantry went over the top. The German front lines were saturated in gas and high explosive and a thick fog covered the battlefield aiding the British. The first wave caught the Germans by surprise and broke straight through their lines, their work being continued by further waves leapfrogging them. At the end of the day an advance of up to eight miles had been made in places, further than during the Somme and Passchendaele; 27,700 Germans had been made casualties including 15,000 prisoners for the loss of 9,000 British.

Fighting continued in the following days but became less effective as German resistance stiffened. By 11 August it had died away as Haig and Rawlinson successfully fought against Foch's desire to renew the attack. Alongside their new tactics the BEF had also learned not to keep attacking once the initial surprise had faded and they would now turn their attention to another sector. By continually switching the focus of attention, the Germans were to be battered into submission through a flurry of blows rather than one knock-out punch. German morale was cracking and Ludendorff referred to the first day of Amiens as 'The black day of the German Army'.

It was now a question of whether the German Army or the home front would collapse first. Following Amiens the Allies erupted into action, in what became known as The Hundred Days campaign as the BEF fought across the Somme regaining the lost ground of spring. Further south the French were in action and to the east the Americans launched their first army scale operation at St-Mihiel. By 2 September Ludendorff had ordered a general retreat to the Hindenburg Line where he had begun the year.

Despite the impressive advance there were still large numbers of British soldiers languishing in prisoner of war camps including fifty-three Torquinians. The breakdown shows which units included local men.

REGIMENT	NUMBER OF SOLDIERS IN POW CAMPS
Devonshire Regiment	13
Worcestershire Regiment	6
Wiltshire Regiment	4
Royal Army Medical Corps	3
Machine Gun Corps, Rifle Brigade, Royal West Kent, Royal Fusiliers, Royal Marines, Royal Navy	2 each
Cheshire, Dorset, Duke of Cornwall Light Infantry, Middlesex, London Rifles, Royal Berkshire, Royal Garrison Artillery, Royal Lancashire Fusiliers, Royal Inniskilling Fusiliers, Royal Warwicks, Somerset, South Wales Borderers, Suffolk, Yorkshire	1 each
Total	**52**

Torquinian Soldiers in German Prisoner of War Camps, October 1918
Source: Torquay Directory, October 16, 1918

Even at this stage of the war the majority of prisoners had been serving in the Devons at the time of their capture suggesting that despite having their presence diluted there were still significant clusters of local men within the Devons.

Despite the recent successes many were still of the opinion that the war would drag into 1919. Haig on the other hand believed that if the Hindenburg Line wasn't carried before winter it would give Germany time to recover. After a heated debate he got his way and the advance continued. Although Haig had been guilty of prolonging offensives in the past, this time his reasoning was absolutely correct. All that now stood between the BEF and the Hindenburg Line was the Canal du Nord, a hundred foot wide in places.

At 5.20am on 27 September four divisions of Canadians infiltrated across the canal in darkness and took the defenders by surprise. The following day Plumer and Second Army, alongside their Belgian allies, recaptured the Passchendaele Ridge and then Messines the following day before advancing eastward to within two miles of Roulers. Ahead of Plumer lay the road to Brussels.

Rawlinson's Fourth Army now launched the epic battle of St Quentin Canal, to the south of the Canal du Nord. A mixed army of Australian, British and Americans crossed the canal and fought their way through the Hindenburg Line before emerging from the maze of trenches into open country. As they looked ahead they could see green untouched farmland. Norman Cliff who had been in the thick of the fighting from Operation Michael onwards described what was motivating the average British soldier during these final months:

'Hope spurred us on, and I am sure the thought struck each one of us that if one's luck held out there was a possibility of surviving – a thought we had dared not entertain hitherto.'

In the south-east, despite impressive early results, the United States' newly launched Meuse-Argonne Offensive was running into trouble. The problems that the Americans were experiencing were similar to the BEF's in 1915/16, giving credence to the argument that the British errors were not solely due to poor leadership. Despite this the offensive was tying down vital German forces and slowly progressing. As the Americans toiled, the BEF were making good their breach of the Hindenburg Line as Cambrai was finally captured on 8 October and to the north Plumer and the Belgians liberated large swathes of Belgium.

In mid-October the town of Le Cateau, famous for its role in 1914, was recaptured and the BEF pushed eastward to the Sambre-Oise Canal where on 4 November they once again defeated the exhausted Germans. At roughly the same time the Americans had finally broken through the Argonne and were advancing on Sedan and Metz alongside the French. After the Battle of the Sambre, sustained German resistance fell away.

On 6 November the last Torquinian to die on the Western Front, Corporal Thomas Bickford, was killed in action and four days later Private Adolphe John Alford died of wounds, the last local man to die in the war.

At 5am on 11 November Germany signed an armistice conceding all the Allies' conditions. It would go into effect at 11am. Fighting continued until the final minutes and soldiers died until the very last seconds. Around 7am Norman Cliff heard the first rumours of the armistice and shortly after was given confirmation:

'It was over! And we were alive! Our hearts leapt. It was almost unbelievable. Thoughts instantly flew home. A weight and strain such as Atlas never imagined rolled off my shoulders, and a spirit of release flew like a bird from my heart. Something snapped in my mind. Mechanically we obeyed the final commands. On the word 'Dismiss!' I rushed back to the billet and amid a din of riotous cheering seized my rifle, equipment and all my belongings and flung the whole lot in the air. Others followed suit. A kind of frenzied madness seized us and we were no longer responsible for our antics and foolery. All the frustration, resentment, exasperation, sorrow, hope and despair had been bottled up for long harrowing years. Sudden relief was bound to cause an explosion.

As suddenly, quietness returned. Feelings welled up that were too deep for expression. A dumbness fell upon us, and a solemn thought mood took over; but not for long. Our excitement could not be contained. I had renounced everything to become Guardsman Cliff "for the duration of the war". The war was over. I was Civilian Cliff again.'

As the final battles were being fought, Canadian soldiers entered Mons where the BEF's war had begun. It was here that it ended. From Amiens to Armistice, 297,765 British soldiers became casualties, roughly the same number as at Passchendaele. Torquay had lost forty men, almost as many as during the *Kaiserschlacht*. However the BEF had finally ascended the learning curve and put together war-winning tactics featuring intense hurricane artillery bombardments, extensive tank and aircraft support and heavily armed mobile infantry acting on their own initiative and led by well-trained officers. For all his faults earlier in the war it had been Haig who actively pushed to finish the war in 1918 and had vigorously driven his subordinates forward during the final battles. The Hundred Days represented the BEF completing its education in modern warfare.

The news arrived in Torquay at 9am onboard HMS *Onyx*:

'It soon spread throughout the harbourside and barely before five past the hour, all the boats lying in the harbour "shrilled out their piercing notes of rejoicing" before a great cheer went up at the RAF headquarters on Haldon Pier…Crowds of joyful and elated people thronged the pavements and streets…For over four long and weary years the beast of war and oppression had stalked the world, and now the beast was dead!

'The New Zealanders based at St Marychurch marched through the town…en route they stopped at Castle Circus and sang one of their famous songs before arriving at the harbourside, where they were greeted by the Mayor standing on one of the balconies of the Queen's Hotel. The Mayor was greeted by cheers before stating that he did not suppose that many of his words would reach them because of the glorious noise from the ships in the harbour. He stated that the New Zealanders had been splendid allies who "coloured our will upon the wretches who sought to establish the domination of the world". And sought to thank them "for their help in accomplishing what must be the most momentous factor in the history of this old planet". Applause erupted from those gathered around before the Mayor lead the men in cheers for Marshal Foch, Sir Douglas Haig, the Prime Minister, King and Queen and then the national anthem was played.'

The celebrations continued well into the night:

'Some parties of soldiers and sailors, aided by girls, marched up and down the streets, singing and cheering. A number of the parties were rather comical in appearances, soldiers and sailors having changed headgear, and being otherwise adorned. A party of New Zealanders went about the town giving exhibitions of a war dance, whilst in the evening two commandeered an electric light standard and went through a number of acrobatic feats a professional performer might envy. Fireworks and rockets were freely discharged.

When evening came on, there was a noticeable indication of the changed state of affairs. The masking had been removed from electrical standards, and when the lights were turned on, the streets presented a dazzlingly-bright appearance. The charge that went from the large concourse of people on the Strand at the change in the lighting was well worth hearing. One set of demonstrators appeared with an effigy of the Kaiser, adorned with a huge Iron Cross, and labelled "Der Tag". Another placard in evidence read "Like the Kaiser we've shut up".'

The armistice assigned territory for each ally to occupy with the British sector around Cologne and Plumer and the Second Army assigned to occupy the area. They marched through Belgium to a rapturous reception and Plumer accompanied King Albert as he marched triumphantly into Brussels. Amongst the soldiers marching into Germany was Norman Cliff, who had also been assigned to the occupation.

In December Plumer took a brief break from his duties and joined Haig the other army commanders in meeting the Prime Minister and the King. He was promoted to the rank of Field-Marshal and made Baron Plumer of Messines and Bilton in the County of York. Haig refused to accept any title until the government committed to providing proper provision for those men disabled in the war.

At home the general election began with the Conservative and Coalition Liberals under Lloyd-George campaigning on their war record and granting 'coalition coupons' to all MPs who had supported them. A rump Liberal Party under Asquith remained to challenge alongside the Labour Party. Colonel Burn was one of those that received a coalition coupon and faced Captain Russell Cooke of the Asquith Liberals and Major Trestrail of Labour. The influence of the war was evident in the fact that all three major candidates were military men.

On 4 December a tribute was paid to the 2nd Devons as the legend of Bois des Buttes continued to grow; from Castle Circus a procession of military and civic figures led a march through the town. The band of the Royal Marines led the way, playing Chopin's 'Funeral March' and behind them was a banner with black letters on a white background saying 'To the glorious memory of the gallant 2nd Devons'. Following the marines came a number of New Zealanders, wounded soldiers, civic figures and all three Parliamentary candidates. Marching through the town, they passed a number of flags flying at half-mast before arriving at the clock tower, while 'Abide with Me' was played. Finally two of the New Zealanders sounded the last post and the ceremony ended with the crowd singing the National Anthem. As the year drew to a close the German submarine *U-92* was brought to the town to shelter from poor weather; the following week another submarine arrived in the town for a longer duration and was moored in the harbour for public viewings.

On 14 December the war-time coalition swept back to power with Lloyd-George remaining Prime Minister. In Torquay, Burn romped home to victory taking 14,058 votes to Trestrail's 4,029 and Cooke's 3,173. That a Labour candidate outpolled a Liberal in Torquay, even a Liberal running against the government, was a sign of the Liberal Party's deep crisis.

Elsewhere another more significant election was held for the right to represent Torre Ward, Mrs V.F. Gresham becoming the first woman to stand for election to Torquay Borough Council. Opposing her was the ex-mayor of Scarborough, William Ball. It was a David vs. Goliath contest but Gresham appeared the more active candidate, debating issues in far more detail. During a rally at Torre Boys' School, Councillor Cawdle spoke in favour of Mrs Gresham, stating that 'years ago he was not in favour of ladies occupying seats on public bodies...The past four years had changed his mind. Women had proven themselves capable in every respect of being fellow citizens with men.' He was not alone in these thoughts. On 27 November the vote was held and a record number of votes were cast including large numbers of women. When the votes were counted

Ball won by 625 votes to 325. Mrs Gresham was unable to attend the count due to illness and in her place stood Lady Acland. She commented that:

> 'For many years she had felt it a scandal that Torquay with its nine wards, had no women on the town council and that Mrs Gresham's attempt had been a bold and brave thing and that no doubt other women would follow.'

Few could argue with her sentiments as Gresham's campaign began a new era in Torquay's political history.

The year 1918 had been a momentous one. When the guns finally stopped firing it had cost Torquay 150 lives, enough to make it the second worst of the war. Amongst those serving in the army the average age of fallen soldiers was just 26.93 years, almost the same as in 1915 which had been heavily influenced by the volunteer boom. The one arm of the armed forces that showed an especially disproportionate average age for those killed was the newly formed RAF. Of the four Torquinians that died serving in it, their average age was just 20.75 years old.

The BEF had ascended the learning curve of modern warfare and by the armistice become arguably the most effective army in the world. Mistakes had been made and many lives needlessly lost but the achievement in creating a mass army from scratch and leading it to victory over the world's premier military power was something to be proud of. The war had been nothing less than a national effort. From the men fighting in the mud, such as Guardsman Norman Cliff, to the women tending to the wounds of injured and maimed soldiers, such as Agatha Christie. They all played their part in achieving victory. Britain and Torquay had come a long way from the days of August 1914 when the council was worrying about whether to cancel a sailing regatta.

Aftermath

For the first time in five years the New Year brought peace. In Germany, Plumer faced a tough winter ensuring that his army and the civilian population were fed. Norman Cliff reflected:

'The people of Cologne welcomed us as rescuers from anarchy. It was a city of hunger and misery. One felt ashamed to see the damage to the lovely cathedral, and even more ashamed to walk about well-fed whilst children begged for food. We were not met with hatred, but with fear, and offered friendly hospitality…we were at once aware that the Huns were not such bestial monsters as we had been led to believe, but human beings sharing the same sufferings and decent feelings as ourselves.'

Plumer managed to secure supplies to feed the poorer citizens but food remained scarce and in March he wrote a letter to Lloyd-George imploring him to release food to the German people. He succeeded and some was allowed to pass through the naval blockade, first for the occupation zone and later for all of Germany. In a sign of how eager the public was for Germany to be harshly treated, some actually criticised Plumer but his actions did much to keep the situation around Cologne stable while Germany collapsed into anarchy. On 21 April he returned to England, his service finally over. At the beginning of May he visited Torquay for the first time in years to receive the freedom of the town and speaking at the occasion he said that he 'appreciated the honour highly as a personal tribute and as a tribute to his troops for the work they had done' and stated that he had spent many happy years as a child growing up in the town.

At roughly the same time, Norman Cliff was finally discharged. Despite his pacifism and hatred for the war, he surprised himself in a discussion with fellow soldiers, stating that if the situation called for it he would fight again. His memoirs do not explain why he took this view other than a strong belief that another such war would never be possible. His return to civilian life was difficult:

'Accompanying my joy, relief and amazement at finding myself still alive – and, the greater miracle, still apparently relatively sane – was a crushing weight of grief for those who had been left to rot in the mud, and a bitter anger over the pitiless way in which their young lives had been thrown away…In fact for twelve months after demobilisation I carried on under a black cloud of neurasthenia, and at the mere mention of the war burst into tears. I was really broken hearted. Only slowly did I recover.'

Cliff's breakdown and subsequent pacifism was not an unusual experience, many demobilised soldiers experienced similar feelings but many also believed that the war had been a necessary measure, despite their own personal privations, and would continue to defend the cause for which it had been fought.

The war had taken a heavy toll. At least 594 Torquinians were killed, the total number probably higher due to the vagaries of record keeping. They served and died across the world: 405 on the Western Front; 41 in the North Sea, 19 in Egypt/Palestine, 15 in

Mesopotamia, 13 at Gallipoli, 11 in the Pacific, 7 in both Italy and India, 6 at Salonika and 2 in East Africa. The remainder dying in hospitals at home.

Of the 505 Torquinians who died serving in the army and whose cause of death was known, 294 were killed in action, 107 died of wounds, 89 died of illness or of long term wounds, 5 died at sea and 1 was killed in an accident. It is also important to note that only 12 per cent of those who served actually died during the war, many hundreds more men returned to the town carrying the scars of the conflict for years to come.

Throughout the war local men served in every branch of the armed forces. Their largest influence was in the Devonshire Regiment and this is reflected in the casualty rates: 159 Torquinians died while serving in the Devons but substantial numbers also served elsewhere, 34 died in the Royal Engineers, 22 in the Artillery, 18 in the London Regiment, 17 in the Somerset Light Infantry, 16 in the Royal Fusiliers, 13 in the Worcestershire Regiment (some being transferred Devons) and many more throughout the army in regiments as exotic as the Imperial Camel Corps and the Chinese Labour Corps.

These men and those that survived were like you and me. At times they were brave, at times selfless and heroic and at other times they could be prone to feelings of fear and self- preservation. They were individuals, each with his own background and story that the war added to or unfortunately brought to a premature end. The average age of a fallen Torquinian was 27.26 years old in the Army, 30.09 years old in Navy and just 20.75 years old in the Air Force. The youngest was Percy James White aged 15 and the oldest were Sergeant Major Joshua Shapcott, Lance Corporal William Mudge and Pioneer Robert Hawkins, all 56. From Edwin Coombes, the first casualty of the war to Corporal Thomas Bickford, the last Torquinian to die in action, they should be remembered for their sacrifice. Dealing with a subject of this size, it has not been possible to draw pen portraits of each soldier in this book but perhaps in the future someone will take up this challenge.

Following the end of the war, the anniversary of the declaration in November now carried far more poignancy, unfortunately the commemorations were ruined by the rain in a typical piece of Torquay weather. A further shake up of the political establishment occurred that month as the first ever Labour councillor for Torquay was elected in Ellacombe Ward. A working class district, this victory was a clear sign of Labour's growing support amongst ex-servicemen and the working classes who were abandoning the Liberals.

With the war over the New Zealand discharge depot wound down throughout 1919. Since their arrival, 30,000 New Zealanders had passed through the town, close to one third of all the Kiwis who served in the war. Men had been departing throughout the year and there now remained only a few stragglers. The rugby team played its final matches before departing, leaving behind a strong legacy; in the coming years a number of New Zealanders returned to play for Torquay and the team was noted as being particularly influenced by the 'colonial' style of play for years to come. A large ceremony was held at Beacon Quay and the Mayor said the final goodbyes to both the soldiers and a large number of local women leaving with the soldiers. A video of this event can be viewed on the British Pathé website.

As the soldiers departed they left behind another legacy, illegitimate births in Torquay had spiked from 39 before their arrival to 59 in 1918 and 81 in 1919, in the final year illegitimate births accounted for 18 per cent of all births. Although a number of these would not have involved New Zealanders, given the paucity of men in town it is likely they contributed a substantial amount, meaning that for the coming years a little part of Torquay was still New Zealand.

For two years Torquay had become a New Zealand beyond the seas providing rest, relaxation and comfort for those men who had done their duty. There exists a small memorial for the fallen in Torquay cemetery, however, in the author's opinion, there should be a far more prominent memorial for the brave men of the NZEF reminding Torquay of the sacrifices they made. Bulford has its giant chalk Kiwi, Torquay should have something equally as recognisable, perhaps next to the Torquay War Memorial, emphasising how the men of Britain and New Zealand stood side by side as part of the greater British Empire.

When it came to commemorating the dead, the government had decided to bury Britain's fallen heroes where they had fallen. Those soldiers that died in the war hospitals in Britain were often buried where they died and as a result Torquay Cemetery contains 136 graves of soldiers from across the Commonwealth including New Zealanders, two Canadians and two Australians. There are no Belgian war graves which suggests the influx of Belgians survived their period in town unscathed or that any Belgian soldiers who died were repatriated.

As for a civic memorial to the dead, the authorities were initially slow to lead. Amongst the earliest suggestions were for a shrine or obelisk; other suggestions included building a hundred houses for working men. By the middle of the year the council had finally taken the lead and was driving fund raising efforts to build the familiar monument in the Princess Gardens and to pay for it by public subscription. Anyone who subscribed could place their loved one's name upon the monument. It was to be designed by Sir Reginald Blomfield and cost more than £2,000, making it one of the most expensive memorials in Devon. When unveiled on 23 April 1921, the memorial was the first to be erected in Devon's major towns.

There is a problem with the memorial for the student of the Great War. As anyone was allowed to place names upon it, the list of soldiers it displays includes a number with no links to Torquay. Sons, grandsons and nephews of Torquay residents, who were neither born in Torquay nor lived in the town, are listed. Although their sacrifice should be remembered they were not strictly Torquinians. Furthermore because of the need to subscribe some of the poorer elements of Torquay could not afford to have their loved one's name on the monument. Single men and those resident in 1914, but with few relatives or friends in the town, are less likely to have been recorded, as are those born in the town but who had since moved away. In creating the list of casualties at the end of this book, the author found 171 fallen Torquinians (born in Torquay or resident in 1914) not listed. It is the author's opinion that with the coming centenary of the war, these names should be added to the memorial to ensure that their sacrifice is not forgotten.

The remembrance of those who had died was not limited to the war memorial. The Bois des Buttes' legend continued to grow and in 1921 a memorial was unveiled near the site of the battle. In the Ypres Salient the Menin Gate was constructed as a memorial to the missing, also designed by Sir Reginald Blomfield. Inside the gate's arch are engraved the names of 54,896 Commonwealth soldiers who died in the Salient and have no known graves. The gate was completed and opened in 1927 with Plumer being present to unveil it, where he reflected on the events nearly a decade past:

'One of the most tragic features of the Great War was the number of casualties reported as "missing, believed killed". To their relatives there must have been added to their grief a tinge of bitterness and a feeling that everything possible had not been done to recover their loved ones' bodies, and give them a reverent burial...A memorial has been erected…and now it can be said of each one in whose honour we are assembled here today..."He is not missing, he is here!"'

Finally at Vimy Ridge where the Canadian nation had been born in a flurry of bullets and shrapnel, the French people granted Canada perpetual use of the highest point of the ridge as a memorial to the men. Due to connections in France, Walter W. Jenkins and Company, based in Upton, was awarded the contract to construct the memorial and another Torquinian Mr W.H. Kendrick was selected to inscribe the names of Canada's fallen upon the monument.

As the memorials began to rise, Torquay was slowly moving on from the war, the erection of the memorials a conscious final act. The war marked the end of Torquay's golden age, which had almost mirrored the Pax Britannica of 1815-1914. The town had lost almost half a decade of growth, the death of nearly 600 men causing a drop in the male population from 17,033 in 1911 to 15,936 in 1921. Following the peace Torquay continued its decline from a premier coastal resort to just another seaside town. By the mid-1930s it was actively seeking the custom of mass market tourism, something it had previously shunned with a passion. Following the Second World War and the emergence of cheap package holidays in the 1960s and 70s the decline hastened. The war also had a devastating effect upon the country as a whole, never again would Britain possess the power or self-confidence she did previously. However despite other nations turning to Fascism in the aftermath, Britain was never enticed and would lead the fight against it in the next war. Fascism did gain one prominent supporter as Colonel Burn joined the British Fascists in 1923, although he soon lost his parliamentary seat. Burn played a prominent role in its early years before dying in 1930, shortly before it merged with Oswald Mosley's New Party to form the British Union of Fascists.

Herbert Plumer's career followed a more conventional path, he became Governor of Malta where he remained until 1924 and after returning to England was offered the position of Governor-General of Australia due to his excellent relationship with the Australian soldiers during the war. Much to the disappointment of the Australians he was forced to turn down the offer due to lacking the financial ability to perform it. Instead he became High Commissioner of Palestine in 1925 until his departure in 1928 when his health began to fail. He died 1932 and was buried in Westminster Abbey near the tomb of the Unknown Soldier. Plumer had been one of the more successful generals of the war, one who understood the limitations of trench warfare and who cared greatly for the condition of his soldiers. While he made mistakes, he was not portrayed as a 'butcher' as many Great War generals were. His funeral attracted a large public attendance, as had Haig's four years earlier which attracted crowds rivalling Churchill's later in the century.

The historian Basil Liddell-Hart, hardly a fan of the war's conduct, summed up Plumer in a revealing quote, stating that Plumer had 'perhaps the nearest approach to military genius in a war singularly devoid of that inspired quality'. Despite his achievements – the stoic defence of Ypres, the Battle of Messines and his trilogy of successes during Passchendaele – Plumer is barely remembered in Torquay. There is no equivalent of the *Plumerlaan*, a street in Ypres. Like the New Zealanders there should be more recognition of Plumer's service, reflecting his role as one of the most able and caring generals of the war, one who was not a 'donkey' but a fallible man struggling to get to grips with a massively changing form of warfare and one that did better than most.

The other prominent figures of Torquay's war lived a varied post war life. The Reverend J.T. Jacob returned to his religious work and dropped out of the historical record. Percy Fawcett returned to his Amazonian explorations, ultimately disappearing without trace in the Amazon jungle in 1925 while searching for the mysterious city of 'Z'. His story has been optioned to make into a movie by none other than Brad Pitt. Norman Cliff's experience turned him into a vociferous opponent of war, he joined the *News Chronicle* in London and in the lead up to the Second World War campaigned for pacifists worldwide to form a *cordon sanitaire* between the opposing armies. From 1946 he became the paper's New Delhi's correspondent and struck up a friendship with Gandhi before dying in peaceful retirement in 1977. Agatha Christie left Torquay during the middle of the war and later became the world's best-selling novelist. Much of her work was directly inspired by her wartime experiences in Torquay.

Although these men and women left behind the most revealing stories of Torquay's experience, every one of the thousands of men and women who served during the war, many quoted in this book, contributed to victory and should each be remembered for their sacrifice. Looking back from the twenty-first century it's easy to characterise the war as a tragic waste, one fought for poor reasons and achieving nothing more than another war. This was not the unanimous view of those who had lived through it. Norman Cliff, hardly a supporter of war, emphasised this:

'How naive we were. Most of us who were volunteers in the 1914-18 war really believed that it would be the last, that our sacrifices would put an end to war forever and make possible a happier future for generations to come. It may seem incredible now, but we honestly believed this and acted accordingly.'

Cliff and others believed it had been worthwhile and had been fought for the defeat of militarism and autocracy. The war had been a moral necessity and Britain had seen it through to a successive conclusion. Many others held negative views of the war but there was not the overwhelming dissatisfaction with that war that is often cited. Instead there was a vibrant debate for decades to come about the worth of the war and the nature of its conduct. By the 1970s, as many of the veterans who had previously defended the war died off, negative views solidified. In Dan Todman's words, the myth of the war and the emphasis upon its most horrific aspects evolved from 'something that some people thought, to something that most people thought, to the point where it was what everyone knew'. Only recently has this been challenged by a more nuanced view closer to the post war situation.

With the hundredth anniversary of the war upon us, it will be remembered in countries spanning the globe in hundreds of different ways. However there is one monument that speaks most tellingly of the sacrifices made by Torquay and why they should never be forgotten. It is not the war memorial on the seafront or the Menin Gate standing silent vigil over Ypres. Instead it lies in a small nondescript war cemetery in the Picardy countryside. There amongst the trees and the birds chirping overhead lie the bodies of 163 men, including five Torquinians, at rest alongside their comrades much as they did in 1916. At the entrance to the cemetery is a small stone memorial that has replaced a previous wooden cross. On the memorial is a simple sentence that summarises the sacrifices of 1914-1918 in a way that few others can:

'The Devonshires held this trench; The Devonshires hold it still.'

Torquay born or resident Casualties

Note: The information included in this appendix was created from a number of sources including C.T Atkinson's *History of the Devonshire Regiment 1914-1919*, the Commonwealth War Graves Commission, the 1911 UK Census, the WO/363 British Army World War One Service Records, the WO/364 British Army World War One Pension Records, Soldiers Died in the Great War: 1914-1919, the Canadian Great War Project and Veterans Affairs Canada (both online) and the Australian War Memorial and Mapping Our Anzacs (both online).

The appendix lists the names of all Torquinian-born or Torquay-resident (in 1914) soldiers that fell during the war. As such it considers the end of the war to be 11/11/1918 and does not contain any deaths beyond this date. The two exceptions to this methodology are the soldiers Cary and Palk, who are listed because of their family's extensive history and landowning within Torquay.

Name / Rank / Soldier Number / Place of Birth / Enlisted (Residence if not the same) / Cause of Death / Theatre / Date / Battalion / Age at Death / Battle died in (if known) / On Torquay War Memorial Y/N?

Devonshire Regiment Casualties (listed by battalion)

Frederick Walter Baker, Private, 9503, Torquay, Totnes (Unknown), Killed in Action, Western Front, 30/10/1914, 1st, 18, N

Ernest Battershill, Private, 3/7134, Torquay, Exeter (Torquay), Killed in Action, Western Front, 15/3/1915, 1st, 17, Western Front (Near Ypres), Y

Harry Ernest Beazley, Private, 9643, Torquay, Newton Abbot (Torquay), Killed in Action, Western Front, 29/10/1914, 1st, Unknown, Y

John Henry Bevan, Private, 8430, Torquay, Torquay (Ashburton), Died of Wounds, Western Front, 20/7/1916, 1st, 28, Battle of the Somme, N

Frederick Benning, Acting Corporal, 5504, Bristol, Torquay, Killed in Action, Western Front, 23/7/1916, 1st, 35, Battle of the Somme, N

Lionel Brough, Private, 22146, Torquay, Newton Abbot (Torquay), Killed in Action, Western Front, 23/4/1917 1st, Unknown, Y

John Cowell, Acting Corporal, 11998, Torquay, Exeter (Torquay), Killed in Action, Western Front, 6/11/1917, 1st, Unknown, Battle of Passchendaele, N

William Albert Crees, Private, 23788, Stoke Gabriel, Torquay, Killed in Action, Western Front, 4/10/1917, 1st, Unknown, Battle of Passchendaele, Y

Joseph Henry Crute, Private, 20608, Torquay, Torquay, Killed in Action, Western Front, 4/10/1917, 1st, 25, Battle of Passchendaele, Y

Frederick Hammond, Private, 21038, Worthing, Newton Abbot (Torquay), Killed in Action, Western Front, 31/8/1916, 1st, 45, Battle of the Somme, N

Frederick Thomas Harvey, Private, 7736, Torquay, Torquay, Killed in Action, Western Front, 3/5/1915, 1st, 28, 2nd Ypres, N

William Henley, Private, 5328, Torquay, Torquay, Killed in Action, Western Front, 6/12/1914, 1st, 37, Western Front (Near Ypres), Y

Victor George Reginald Hole, Private, 14625, Torquay, Paignton (Unknown), Killed in Action, Western Front, 23/4/1917, 1st, Unknown, Battle of Arras, Y

George Henry Lale, Private, 9539, Torquay, Exeter (Torquay), Died, Western Front, 14/12/1914, 1st, 20, Western Front, N

William Albert Henry Mathers, Acting Corporal, 7610, Torquay, Torquay, Died of Wounds, Western Front, 24/6/1915, 1st, 30, Western Front (Near Ypres), Y

Wilfred Matthews, Private, 14082, Torquay, Paignton (Torquay), Died, Western Front, 24/12/1916, 1st, 20, Western Front, N

Frank Millman, Private, 24600, Liskeard. Exeter (Torquay), Died of Wounds, Western Front, 22/8/1918, 1st, Unknown, Hundred Days, Y

Frederick Thomas Ould, Private, 11482, Torquay, Exeter (Torquay), Killed in Action, Western Front, 29/4/1915, 1st, Unknown, 2nd Ypres, Y

Walter Parnell, Private, 42694, Bolton - Cornwall, Newton Abbot (Torquay), Killed in Action, Western Front, 4/10/1917, 1st, 33, Battle of Passchendaele, Y

Frederick Charles Penwell, Private, 11281, Paignton, Exeter (Torquay), Killed in Action, Western Front, 3/9/1916, 1st, 20, Battle of the Somme, N

Henry Powell, Private, 7036, Torquay, Exeter (Torquay), Died of Wounds, Western Front, 29/10/1914, 1st, 32, 1914, Y

Sydney Pym, Private, 15914, Torquay, Exeter (Torquay), Killed in Action, Western Front, 25/9/1916, 1st, Unknown, Battle of the Somme, Y

Henry Percival Rice, Private, 21287, Torquay, Torquay, Died of Wounds, Western Front, 8/9/1916, 1st, 39, Battle of the Somme, Y

Albert William Richards, Corporal, 18659, Newton Poppleford, Exeter (Torquay), Killed in Action, Western Front, 9/5/1917, 1st, 21, Battle of Arras, Y

Frederick John Routley, Corporal, 7437, Ashburton, Ashburton (Torquay), Killed in Action, Western Front, 24/10/1914, 1st, 30, 1914, Y (as Routhley)

Walter John Rowe, Private, 3/7017, Torquay, Exeter (Torquay), Died of Wounds, Western Front, 26/9/1916, 1st, 21, Battle of the Somme, Y

Thomas Smith, Private, 14953, Castlebar - County Mayo, Exeter (Torquay), Died of Wounds, Western Front, 7/5/1915, 1st, 53, 2nd Ypres, Y

Herman Owen Stentiford, Private, 3/6642, Torquay, Exeter (Unknown), Killed in Action, Western Front, 29/8/1916, 1st, 24, Battle of the Somme, Y

Charles Henry Stone, Acting Corporal, 9268, Torquay, Exeter (Torquay), Killed in Action, Western Front, 4/9/1916, 1st, 23, Battle of the Somme, Y

Reginald Warren, Private, 7015, Torquay, Exeter (Torquay), Killed in Action, Western Front, 26/4/1915, 1st, 17, 2nd Ypres, Y

James White, Private, 31156, Avonwick, Torquay, Died of Wounds, Western Front, 23/6/1918, 1st , 27, Western Front, N

George Winsor, Private, 8559, Torquay, Exeter (Torquay), Killed in Action, Western Front, 9/5/1917, 1st, Unknown, Battle of Arras, Y

Wilfred Bagwell, Sergeant, 7537, Kingskerswell, Exeter (Torquay), Died of Wounds, Western Front, 21/12/1914, 2nd, 29, 1914, N

William Bagwell, Private, 11244, Torquay, Exeter (Torquay), Died of Wounds, Western Front, 15/3/1915, 2nd, 19, Western Front, Y

Ernest Beazley, Private, 3/7100, Torquay, Exeter (Torquay), Killed in Action, Western Front, 27/10/1916, 2nd, Unknown, Battle of the Somme, Y (as F)

William James Blight, Private, 71158, Unknown, Newton Abbot (Torquay), Died, Home, 21/4/1918, 2nd, 19, Y

Frank Hilton Blunt, Private, 8346, Torquay, Devonport (Torquay), Died of Wounds, Western Front, 21/10/1916, 2nd, Unknown, Battle of the Somme, Y

James Frederick Bourhill, Corporal, 33173, Edmonton - London, Torquay, Killed in Action, Western Front, 31/7/1917, 2nd, 21, Battle of Passchendaele, Y

Sydney B. Bowden, Private, 11273, Ashburton, Exeter (Torquay), Killed in Action, Western Front, 10/3/1915, 2nd, Unknown, Battle of Neuve Chapelle, Y

Alfred Brown, Private, 13139, Torquay, Porth, Glam (Torquay), Killed in Action, Western Front, 12/3/1915, 2nd, 29, Battle of Neuve Chapelle, Y

Vincent Cahill, Private, 3/7535, Torquay, Exeter (Torquay), Killed in Action, Western Front, 13/3/1915, 2nd, 40, Battle of Neuve Chapelle, Y

Fred England, Private, 16684, Torquay, Torquay, Killed in Action, Western Front, 18/7/1916, 2nd, 21, Battle of the Somme, Y

William Fuller, Acting Corpora, 8128, Torquay, Exeter (Unknown), Killed in Action, Western Front, 31/5/1915, 2nd, 25, Western Front, N

John Henry Green, Private, 29683, Torquay, Torquay, Killed in Action, Western Front, 23/3/1917, 2nd, Unknown, Western Front, Y

Augustine Hannaford, Private, 3/7532, Torquay, Exeter (Torquay), Killed in Action, Western Front, 1/7/1916, 2nd, Unknown, Battle of the Somme, Y

Frederick William Henry Hannaford, Acting Corporal, 290440, Torquay, Exeter (Torquay), Died, Western Front, 8/8/1918, 2nd, 21, Hundred Days, Y

Ernest John Hatton, Sergeant, 3/5673, Torquay, Newton Abbot (Torquay), Killed in Action, Western Front, 1/7/1916, 2nd, 27, Battle of the Somme, Y

Charles Thomas James, Private, 29679, Torquay, Torquay, Killed in Action, Western Front, 30/11/1917, 2nd, 36, Western Front (Near Ypres), Y

Albert John Langdon, Private, 3/5789, Paignton, Torquay, Died of Wounds, Western Front, 26/2/1915, 2nd, Unknown, Western Front, Y

Leo Jacob Langwasser, Private, 3/6829, Newton Abbot, Exeter (Torquay), Killed in Action, Western Front, 1/7/1916, 2nd, 19, Battle of the Somme, Y

William Lavers, Private, 3/7285, Newton Abbot, Exeter (Torquay), Died of Wounds, Western Front, 31/10/1916, 2nd, 45, Battle of the Somme, N

John Phillips Linton, Private, 16937, Plymouth, Torquay, Died of Wounds, Western Front, 14/8/1916, 2nd, 28, Battle of the Somme, Y

Roy Alexander McMorran, Corporal, 20514, Unknown, Torquay, Killed in Action, Western Front, 31/7/1917, 2nd, 20, Battle of Passchendaele, Y

Alfred Manning, Private, 15274, Torquay, Exeter (Torquay), Killed in Action, Western Front, 10/8/1917, 2nd, 19, Battle of Passchendaele, Y

Harold E. Marchant, 2nd Lieutenant, N/A, Plymouth, Unknown (Torquay), Killed in Action, Western Front, 5/6/1916, 2nd, 19, Western Front, Y

Charles Martin, Private, 11419, Unknown, Torquay, Killed in Action, Western Front, 14/11/1915, 2nd, Unknown, Western Front, Y

Bertie Moore, Private, 6962, Torquay, Exeter (Barnstaple), Killed in Action, Western Front, 6/5/1917, 2nd, Unknown, Western Front, N

Thomas Morris, Private, 3/6515, Torquay, Torquay, Killed in Action, Western Front, 18/12/1914, 2nd, Unknown, 1914, Y

William Ernest Ockford, Private, 204887, Torquay, Poole (?), Killed in Action, Western Front, 31/5/1918, 2nd, 38, *Kaiserschlacht* (Blücher-Yorck), N

Frederick Thomas Peters, Private, 203283, Torquay, Newton Abbot (Torquay), Killed in Action, Western Front, 21/6/1917, 2nd, 19, Western Front (Near Ypres), Y

Frederick Robert Redwood, Corporal, 9336, Torquay, Torquay, Killed in Action, Western Front, 1/4/1918, 2nd, 27, *Kaiserschlacht* (Michael), Y

Charles Shute, Private, 8800, Torquay, Torquay, Killed in Action, Western Front, 11/3/1915, 2nd, 26, Battle of Neuve Chapelle, Y

Frederick Squire, Private, 11263, Torquay, Exeter (Torquay), Killed in Action, Western Front, 10/5/1915, 2nd, 21, Western Front, Y

Joseph Tanner, Private, 6402, Torquay, Torquay, Killed in Action, Western Front, 1/7/1916, 2nd, 43, Battle of the Somme, Y

Jack Edward Watts, Corporal, 8313, Torquay, Exeter (Torquay), Killed in Action, Western Front, 9/5/1915, 2nd, 27, Battle of Aubers Ridge, Y

Charles Henry Weeks, Private, 3/6362, Torquay, Torquay, Killed in Action, Western Front, 14/4/1917, 2nd, Unknown, Western Front, N

William R. Weeks, Acting Corporal, 290208, Torquay, Torquay, Died of Wounds, Western Front, 16/10/1918, 2nd, 21, Hundred Days, Y

Thomas Charles Widdecombe, Private, 9870, Torquay, Exeter (Torquay), Died of Wounds, Western Front, 14/12/1914, 2nd, 19, 1914, Y

George Henry Hammond, Drummer, 8330, Torquay, London (Torquay), Died, Home, 11/12/1915, 3rd, 27, Y

John Horsewell, Private, 14930, Torquay, Exeter (Torquay), Died, Home, 29/12/1914, 3rd, 38, Y (as Horswell)

Alfred Wakeham, Private, 15614, Torquay, Exeter (Torquay), Died, Home, 30/12/1916, 3rd, 30, Y

William Frederick Vine, Acting Corporal, Newton Abbot, Exeter (Torquay), Died, Home, 3/7/1915, 3rd, Unknown, Y

Joseph Leonard Bastard, Private, 5001, Unknown, Newton Abbot (Torquay), Killed in Action, Mesopotamia, 3/2/1917, 1/4th, Unknown, Mesopotamian Front, Y

George Buckpitt, Private, 5650, Unknown, Newton Abbot (Torquay), Killed in Action, Mesopotamia, 3/2/1917, 1/4th, Unknown, Mesopotamian Front, Y

Harry Lipscombe, Private, 3223, Torquay, Exeter (Unknown), Died, Egypt, 1/5/1916, 2/4th, 25, N

Herbert Andrews, Private, 1936, Torquay, Plymouth (Torquay), Died, India, 10/12/1914, 1/5th, Unknown, Y

Arthur Stanley Ayshford, Private, 69106, Torquay, Exeter (Torquay), Killed in Action, Western Front, 30/8/1918, 1/5th, 28, Hundred Days, Y

Walter Albert Frank Bond, Sergeant, 8688, Torquay, Exeter (Torquay), Killed in Action, Western Front, 13/9/1918, 1/5th, Unknown, Hundred Days, Y

Reginald John Bulleid, Private, 241398, Torquay, Newton Abbot (Torquay), Killed in Action, Western Front, 20/6/1918, 1/5th, 20, Western Front, Y

Cecil John Chudley, Private, 240757, Unknown, Newton Abbot (Torquay), Killed in Action, Palestine, 23/11/1917, 1/5th, 23, Battle of Jerusalem, Y

Gerald Frank Thomas Crook, Private, 2250, Torquay, Plymouth (Torquay), Died, Mesopotamia, 19/1/1917, 1/5th, 27, Y

Charles Gerrard Deane, Private, 2491, Ashwick, Somerset, Torquay, Died, India, 14/12/1914, 1/5th, Unknown, Y

Arthur William D. Grater, Private, 241401, Highampton, Devon, Newton Abbot (Torquay), Killed in Action, Western Front, 27/9/1918, 1/5th, 21, Hundred Days (Canal du Nord), Y

David John Muir, Private, 241006, Barnstaple, Plymouth (Torquay), Killed in Action, Western Front, 28/7/1918, 5th, 21, *Kaiserschlacht* (Second Marne), Y

Thomas Henry Perring, Private, 315279, Torquay, Plymouth (Unknown), Killed in Action, Palestine, 13/11/1917, 1/5th, 36, Battle of Mughar Ridge, N

John Snell, Private, 46843, Torquay, Exeter (Torquay), Killed in Action, Palestine, 12/3/1918, 1/5th, Unknown, Second Action of Es Sal, Y

William Snell, Private, 240096, Torquay, Moretonhampsted (Torquay), Killed in Action, Palestine, 13/11/1917, 1/5th, 34, Battle of Mughar Ridge, N

Reginald Morris Willis, Private, 3023, Unknown, Newton Abbot (Torquay), Died, Egypt, 17/6/1916, 5th, Unknown, N/A, Y

George Ernest Chapman, Private, 202816, Torquay, Plymouth (Unknown), Died, Mesopotamia, 11/3/1918, 1/6th, 21, Y

Henry Field, Private, 3804, Torquay, Exeter (Torquay), Killed in Action, Mesopotamia, 8/3/1916, 1/6th, 25, Siege of Kut, Y

Edward John Bassett, Private, 11980, Torquay, Newton Abbot (Unknown), Killed in Action, Western Front, 1/7/1916, 8th, 33, Battle of the Somme, Y (as J.E)

Benjamin Blackmore, Corporal, 9616, Torquay, Torquay, Killed in Action, Western Front, 4/10/1917, 8th, Unknown, Battle of Passchendaele, Y

William Browning, Private, 11525, Dawlish, Exeter (Torquay), Killed in Action, Western Front, 1/7/1916, 8th, Unknown, Battle of the Somme, Y

Wilfred George Chamberlain, Corporal, 33154, Torquay, Torquay, Killed in Action, Western Front, 26/10/1917, 8th, 25, Battle of Passchendaele, Y

Frederick Coleman, Sergeant, 10711, Torquay Exeter (Torquay), Killed in Action, Western Front, 25/9/1915, 8th, Unknown, Battle of Loos, Y

John Coles, Private, 26138, Topsham, Torquay, Died, Home, 10/12/1916, 8th, 27, N

Wyndham Archibald Cory, Private, 205065, Unknown, Newton Abbot (Torquay), Killed in Action, Western Front, 4/10/1917, 8th, 34, Battle of Passchendaele, Y (as Corey)

William Arthur Court, Private, 21022, Plymouth, Newton Abbot (Torquay), Killed in Action, Western Front, 28/3/1917, 8th, 22, Western Front, Y

James Henry H. Coulman, Private, 21637, Torquay, Torquay, Killed in Action, Western Front, 26/10/1917, 8th, 29, Battle of Passchendaele, Y

John Burgoyne Ellicott, Private, 45656, Torquay, Exeter (Moreton Bishop), Died of

Wounds, Western Front, 10/5/1917, 8th, 23, Battle of Arras, N

Cyril Elson, 10767, Torquay, Exeter (Torquay), Killed in Action, Western Front, 25/9/1915, 8th, Unknown, Battle of Loos, Y

Ernest George Fragall, Private, 16469, Unknown, Exeter (Torquay), Died of Wounds, Western Front, 5/10/1917, 8th, Unknown, Battle of Passchendaele, N

Edmond Percy Mabin Goss, Private, 10907, Torquay, Devonport (Torquay), Died, Italy, 7/10/1918, 8th, Unknown, Y

Graham Harvey, Corporal, 33149, Torquay, Torquay, Killed in Action, Western Front, 26/10/1917, 8th, Unknown, Battle of Passchendaele, Y

Robert Augustus Lavers, Private, 15825, Torquay, Barnsley (Unknown), Killed in Action, Western Front, 26/9/1915, 8th, 23, Battle of Loos, Y

Hugh Lear, Private, 11906, Torquay, Exeter (Torquay), Killed in Action, Western Front, 25/9/1915, 8th, 20, Battle of Loos, Y

William John Thomas Lewis, Sergeant, 7976, Torquay, Exeter (Unknown), Killed in Action, Western Front, 1/5/1916, 8th, Unknown, Western Front, N

Felix Courtenay Lockyer, 2nd Lieutenant, N/A, Highworth – Wiltshire, Unknown (Torquay), Killed in Action, Western Front, 12/2/1917, 8th, 21, Western Front, Y

John Martin, Sergeant, 9006, Torquay, Exeter (Ottery St. Mary), Killed in Action, Western Front, 4/9/1916, 8th, 27, Battle of the Somme, N

John Francis Martyn, Lance Corporal, 23171, Unknown, Torquay, Died of Wounds, Western Front, 6/10/1917, 8th, 20, Battle of Passchendaele, Y

Sidney George Moore, Private, 14511, Torquay, Exeter (Torquay), Killed in Action, Western Front, 25/9/1915, 8th, 23, Battle of Loos, Y

Frederick Nickells, Private, 30598, Torquay, Torquay, Killed in Action, Western Front, 24/4/1917, 8th, Unknown, Battle of Arras, Y

Percy Palmer, Private, 11892, Torquay, Exeter (Torquay), Killed in Action, Western Front, 25/9/1915, 8th, Unknown, Battle of Loos, Y

William James Rendell, Private, 14514, Torquay, Exeter (Torquay), Died of Wounds, Home, 6/8/1916, 8th, 25, Y

William Henry Rowe, Private, 40859, Blackawton, Torquay, Killed in Action, Western Front, 28/3/1917, 8th, Unknown, Western Front, N

Ernest Edward Scott, Private, 10715, Torquay, Exeter (Torquay), Killed in Action, Western Front, 25/9/1915, 8th, 29, Battle of Loos, Y

Herbert Southcott, Private, 33467, Unknown, Torquay, Killed in Action, Western Front, 23/4/1917, 8th, Unknown, Battle of Arras, Y

Richard Harold Sprague, Private, 10465, Torquay, Exeter (Torquay), Killed in Action, Western Front, 25/9/1915, 8th, 24, Battle of Loos, Y

John Walling, Private, 20853, Unknown, Newton Abbot (Torquay), Died of Wounds, Home, 24/9/1916, 8th, Unknown, Y

James William Wyatt, Private, 10108, Torquay, Exeter (Torquay), Died, Italy, 20/7/1918, 8th, 24, Y

John Henry Gooding, Private, 14345, Ugborough, Exeter (Torquay), Killed in Action, Western Front, 8/11/1915, 8th, Unknown, Western Front, Y

Frederick Beare, Private, 14413, Torquay, Exeter (Torquay), Killed in Action, Western

Front, 30/9/1915, 9th, Unknown, Battle of Loos, Y

Alfred Bickford, Private, 78115, Unknown, Exeter (Torquay), Killed in Action, Western Front, 4/11/1918, 9th, Unknown, Hundred Days, Y

Alfred Henry Bryant, Private, 9433, Plymouth, Exeter (Torquay), Killed in Action, Western Front, 2/4/1917, 9th, 22, Western Front, N

Frederick Edward Burton, Private, 12952, Torquay, Barry, Died of Wounds, Western Front, 18/10/1915, 9th, 17, Western Front, N

Lancelot Sulyarde Robert Cary, 2nd Lieutenant, N/A, India, Unknown, Killed in Action, Western Front, 20/7/1916, 9th, 24, Battle of the Somme, Y

Frank Albert Cogan, Private, 15466, Torquay, Dartmouth (Torquay), Died of Wounds, Western Front, 15/6/1917, 9th, 22, Western Front, Y

Ernest Boucher Coombe, Private, 11797, Torquay, Poplar, London, Died of Wounds, Western Front, 11/11/1915, 9th, Unknown, Western Front, N

Percival Joseph Endacott, Private, 21166, Torquay, Newton Abbot (Torquay), Killed in Action, Western Front, 6/9/1916, 9th, Unknown, Battle of the Somme, N

Sidney Hooper Fedrick, Private, 20034, Pontypridd, Exeter (Torquay), Killed in Action, Western Front, 1/7/1916, 9th, 18, Battle of the Somme, Y

Frederick Gile, Private, 17090, Torquay, Torquay, Killed in Action, Western Front, 6/9/1916, 9th, Unknown, Battle of the Somme, Y (as Gill)

Thomas Richard Gooding, Private, 14879, Torquay, Paignton (Torquay), Died of Wounds, Western Front, 2/7/1916, 9th, Unknown, Battle of the Somme, N

William Henry Harwood, Private, 26523, Gibraltar, Newton Abbot (Torquay), Died of Wounds, Western Front, 5/11/1917, 9th, 36, Battle of Passchendaele, Y

Phillip John Heaward, Private, 28822, Newton Abbot, Torquay, Killed in Action, Western Front, 26/10/1917, 9th, Unknown, Battle of Passchendaele, Y

Norman Hicks Hingston, Sergeant, 15450, Torquay, Exeter (Torquay), Died of Wounds, Western Front, 10/10/1918, 9th, Unknown, Hundred Days, Y

William Alfred Holding, Private, 11715, Torquay, Cardiff (Torquay), Killed in Action, Western Front, 6/9/1916, 9th, 36, Battle of the Somme, Y

Henry Francis Kernick, Private, 26172, Torquay, Newton Abbot (Unknown), Killed in Action, Western Front, 26/10/1917, 9th, Unknown, Battle of Passchendaele, N

Lawrence Henry Martin, Private, 26525, Torquay, Torquay, Killed in Action, Western Front, 26/10/1917, 9th, Unknown, Battle of Passchendaele, N

William Owen Mayers, Lance Corporal, 16143, Torquay, Plymouth (Unknown), Killed in Action, Western Front, 1/7/1916, 9th, 37, Battle of the Somme, Y

Reginald Orsman, Private, 18773, Torquay, Dumbarton, Killed in Action, Western Front, 1/7/1916, 9th, 19, Battle of the Somme, N

Walter Ernest Payne, Private, 29719, Marldon, Newton Abbot (Torquay), Killed in Action, Western Front, 26/10/1917, 9th, 21, Battle of Passchendaele, Y

William Penwill, Private, 25865, Torquay, Aberystwyth (Unknown), Died of Wounds, Western Front, 7/5/1917, 9th, 31, Battle of Arras, N

Audley St. John Perkins, Lieutenant, N/A, Taunton, Unknown (Torquay), Killed in Action, Western Front, 2/4/1917, 9th, 33, Western Front, Y

Albert Ernest Phillips, Private, 14414, Plymouth, Exeter (Torquay), Died of Wounds,

Western Front, 4/7/1916, 9th, Unknown, Battle of the Somme, Y

George Roscorla, Private, 45781, Unknown, Liskeard (Torquay), Killed in Action, Western Front, 10/10/1917, 9th, Unknown, Battle of Passchendaele, N

Bertram George Ryder, Corporal, 17079, Kingsbridge, Newton Abbot (Torquay), Died of Wounds, Western Front, 11/5/1917, 9th, 28, Battle of Arras, Y

Harry W. Snow, Private, 20862, Exmouth, Newton Abbot (Torquay), Killed in Action, Western Front, 6/9/1916, 9th, Unknown, Battle of the Somme, Y

Vicenzo Spacagna, 30034, Cervard, Italy, Exeter (Torquay), Killed in Action, Western Front, 7/5/1917, 9th, 19, Battle of Arras, Y

George Rose Stone, Private, 14932, Torquay, Exeter (Torquay), Died, Home, 9/6/1918, 9th, 40, Y

Alfred Edgar Willing, Private, 11724, Torquay, Cardiff (Merthyr), Killed in Action, Western Front, 30/9/1915, 9th, 29, Battle of Loos, N

John Henry Beer, Private, 14044, Torquay, Exeter (Torquay), Died of Wounds, Salonika, 25/11/1916, 10th, 29, Salonika Front, Y

Francis George Damerell, Private, 12008, Torquay, Exeter (Unknown), Killed in Action, Salonika, 25/4/1917, 10th, 20, 2nd Battle of Doiran, Y

Frederick Charles Gater, Private, 12730, Exeter, Cardiff (Torquay), Died, Salonika, 5/7/1916, 10th, 19, Salonika Front, N

Albert Edward Land, Private, 17937, Torquay, Paignton (Unknown), Killed in Action, Salonika, 20/2/1917, 10th, 28, Salonika Front, Y

Frank Henry Steer, Private, 24147, Torquay, Newton Abbot (Torquay) Killed in Action, Salonika, 25/4/1917, 10th, 18, 2nd Battle of Doiran, Y

Stanley Reed, Lance Corporal, 16687, Torquay, Torquay, Died, Home, 25/4/1916, 11th, 21, Y

Ernest Edward Boyce, Acting Lance Corporal, 345940, Torquay, Paignton (Torquay), Killed in Action, Palestine, 3/12/1917, 16th, 29, Battle of Jerusalem, Y

William J. Truman, Corporal, 290222, Torquay, Torquay, Killed in Action, Palestine, 3/12/1917, 16th, Unknown, Battle of Jerusalem, Y

William Julian Nisbet Warry, Private, 21843, Torquay, Exeter (Newton Abbot), Died, Home, 19/5/1916, 10th Infantry Works Company, Unknown, N

Other Regiments

Adolphe John Alford, Private, 57837, Beer, Exeter (Torquay), Died of Wounds, Home, 10/11/1918, 2/8th Worcestershire, 19, N/A, Y

George Alford, Driver, T3/027289, Torquay, Exeter (Torquay), Killed in Action, Mesopotamia, 4/7/1916, Royal Army Service Corps, 36, Mesopotamian Campaign, Y

Harold Cecil Allcorn, Rifleman, 592050, Heathfield – Sussex, Unknown (Torquay), Died, Western Front, 12/6/1917, 18th London Regiment (London Irish Rifles), 19, Western Front (Near Ypres), Y

Percy John Allen, Rifleman, B/201454, Torquay, Liverpool (Torquay), Killed in Action, Western Front, 30/10/1917, 1/28th Rifle Brigade, Unknown, Battle of Passchendaele, Y

Frederick Thomas Andrews, Private, 459432, Torquay, Torquay, Killed in Action, Western Front, 30/11/1917, Royal Army Medical Corps, 25th Field Ambulance, 23,

Western Front (Near Ypres), Y

Robert Henry Andrews, Bombardier, 1473, Torquay, Exeter (Paignton), Killed in Action, Western Front, 19/7/1916, Royal Field Artillery, 23, Battle of the Somme, N

Matthew Anstis, Private, 6305, Torquay, Torquay, Killed in Action, Western Front, 8/10/1918, 5th Connaught Rangers, Unknown, Hundred Days, Y

John Armin, Private, G/21035, Torquay, Newton Abbot (Torquay), Killed in Action, Western Front, 23/7/1917, 1st The Queen's Own Royal West Kent, Unknown, Western Front, Y

Ernest Ash, Private, 492163, Torquay, London, Killed in Action, Western Front, 9/4/1917, 1/13th London (Kensington), 40, Battle of Arras, Y

Thomas Avery, Private, 40526, Torquay, Mountain Ash (Unknown), Killed in Action, Western Front, 22/11/1917, 2/4th York and Lancaster, Unknown, Western Front, N

William Henry Palmer Babbage, Sapper, 4074, Torquay, Torquay, Killed in Action, Western Front, 28/4/1915, Royal Engineers, 27th Wessex Div. Signal Company, 53, 2nd Ypres, Y

Harry Prout Badcott, Private, 69717, Torquay, Newton Abbot (Torquay), Killed in Action, Western Front, 21/3/1918, 2nd/2nd Londons, Unknown, Kaiserschlacht (Michael), Y

Sidney Ernest Baker, Sapper, 59300, Coombe-in-Teignhead, Exeter (Torquay), Died, Western Front, 15/6/1917, Royal Engineers, 78th Field Company, 38, Western Front, Y

Mark Christopher Ball, Lieutenant, N/A, Unknown, Unknown (Torquay), Died of Wounds, Western Front, 9/4/1918, Royal Engineers, 231st Field Company, 20, Kaiserschlacht (Georgette), Y

Richard Anthony Ball, Lieutenant, N/A, Unknown, Torquay, Killed in Action, Western Front, 10/7/1916, 2/8th Worcestershire, 20, Battle of the Somme, Y

Samuel Albert Ball, Private, 26955, Ashcombe, Newton Abbot (Torquay), Killed in Action, Western Front, 21/3/1918, 2nd Wiltshire, 33, Kaiserschlacht (Michael), Y

Charles Bandfield, Sergeant, T4/035471, Torquay, Bodmin (St Germans, Cornwall), Killed in Action, Western Front, 21/7/1917, Royal Army Service Corps, 35, Western Front (Near Ypres), N

Rev. Edward Walter Barker, Chaplain 4th Class, N/A, Unknown, Unknown (Torquay), Died of Wounds, Western Front, 18/3/1918, Army Chaplains Department, 30, Western Front, N

George Barrett, Private, 51277, Torquay, Newton Abbot (Torquay), Killed in Action, Western Front, 29/10/1918, 8th King's Liverpool, Unknown, Hundred Days, Y

Thomas John Bartlett, Driver, 62083, Torquay, Exeter (Torquay), Died of Wounds, Western Front, 25/11/1915, Royal Field Artillery, 47th Brigade Ammunition Column, Unknown, Western Front (Near Ypres), Y

Harry Bastin, Private, 302680, Sidmouth, Exeter (Torquay), Killed in Action, Western Front, 22/4/1918, 12th Royal Scots, 19, Kaiserschlacht (Georgette), Y

Thomas Reginald Bawden, Private, 33809, Torquay, Gloucester (Torquay), Killed in Action, Western Front, 30/9/1918, 1/5th Loyal North Lancashire, 26, Hundred Days, Y

Nigel William Francis Baynes, Major, N/A, Torquay, Unknown, Died, Home, 20/3/1915, 1st Gloucestershire, 37, Western Front, Y (as N. W. E.)

John Beacon, Private, 40015, Sittingbourne, Newton Abbot (Torquay), Died of Wounds, Western Front, 4/9/1918, 1st Somerset Light Infantry, 19, Hundred Days, Y

Harry Reginald Beare, Driver, 192109, Torquay, Newton Abbot (Torquay), Died of Illness, Western Front, 16/10/1917, Royal Field Artillery, 62nd Brigade, 29, Western Front, Y

Ernest Alfred Beer, Private, 8636, Torquay, Exeter (Torquay), Died of Wounds, Western Front, 9/5/1917, Royal Army Medical Corps, 12th Field Ambulance, Unknown, Western Front, Y

Frank George Bell, Sapper, 510182, Torquay, Torquay, Died, Home, 7/3/1917, Royal Engineers - 508th (Wessex) Reserve Field Company, 28, Y

C. A. Bellamy, Pioneer, 110600, Unknown, Unknown (Torquay), Died, Home, 6/4/1918Royal Engineers - Depot Labour Battalion, Unknown, Y

Thomas Bennett, Private, 311211, Torquay, Dumfries (Unknown), Died, Egypt, 8/9/1917, 1/7th Northumberland Fusiliers, Unknown, N

William Joseph Bennett, Private, 74446, Torquay, Paignton (Unknown), Died, East Africa, 15/2/1918, Royal Army Medical Corps, Unknown, East Africa Campaign, N

Edgar Bickford, Private, 38520, Torquay, Exeter (Torquay), Killed in Action, Western Front, 1/7/1918, 2nd Highland Light Infantry, 33, Kaiserschlacht, N

Thomas Bickford, Corporal, 534322, Torquay, Hounslow (Acton Vale), Killed in Action, Western Front, 6/11/1918, 15th London, 36, Hundred Days, N

Edgar Duncan George Bird, Private, 8961, Torquay, Exeter (Torquay), Killed in Action, Western Front, 11/4/1917, 3rd Dragoon Guards, 20, Battle of Arras, Y

Henry Bishop, Private, 45017, Torquay, Exeter (Unknown), Killed in Action, Western Front, 15/10/1918, 1st Royal Inniskilling Fusiliers, 19, Hundred Days, Y

Percy Bishop, Private, SP/2791, Torquay, Exeter (Torquay), Died of Wounds, Western Front, 29/7/1916, 24th Royal Fusiliers, Unknown, Battle of the Somme, Y

Thomas Bishop, Private, 27251, Torquay, Newton Abbot (Torquay), Killed in Action, Western Front, 23/4/1917, 2nd Hampshire, 37, Battle of Arras, Y

John Robin Blacker, 2nd Lieutenant, N/A, Unknown, Torquay, Killed in Action, Western Front, 28/9/1915, 1st Coldstream Guards, 18, Battle of Loos, Y (as Blackler)

Ernest Daniel Blackler, Pioneer, 214608, Torquay, Tiverton (Unknown), Died of Wounds, Western Front, 12/7/1917, Royal Engineers, Unknown, Western Front (Near Ypres), Y

James Edwin Blackler, Rifleman, 305956, Torquay, Newton Abbot (Torquay), Killed in Action, Western Front, 11/10/1918, 3/5th London Regiment (London Rifle Brig.), 19, Hundred Days, Y

Harold George Blake, Sapper, 551314, Unknown, Unknown (Torquay), Died, Home, 15/3/1918, Royal Engineers - Railway Troops (Longmoor), 29, N

Frank Bolt, Driver, 4073, Unknown, Torquay, Died of Wounds, Western Front, 25/4/1915, Royal Engineers, Wessex Division Signal Company, Unknown, 2nd Ypres, Y

Percival David Bolt, Rifleman, P/1087, Torquay, London, Killed in Action, Western Front, 3/9/1916, 16th Rifle Brigade, Unknown, Battle of the Somme, N

William Henry Bolt, Guardsman, 26857, Torquay, Newton Abbot (Unknown), Killed in Action, Western Front, 12/10/1917, 1st Grenadier Guards, 30, Battle of Passchendaele, Y

Ernest Edward Bond, Private, 107336, Torquay, Exeter (Torquay), Killed in Action, Western Front, 9/4/1918, Machine Gun Corps, 55th Battalion, 29, Kaiserschlacht, Y

Albert Henry Bowden, Private, 42264, Torquay, South Molton (Molland), Died of Wounds, Home, 1/5/1918, 2nd Yorkshire, Unknown, Y

Hebert Edward Bowden, Private, 55922, Torquay, Exeter (Unknown), Died of Wounds, Western Front, 23/8/1918, 12/13th Battalion Northumberland Fusiliers 29, Hundred Days, Y

Joseph Henry Bowden, Private, 50585, Torquay, Newton Abbot (Torquay), Killed in Action, Western Front, 20/9/1918, 10th Royal Warwickshire, 18, Hundred Days, Y

Leonard George Bowden, Lance Corporal, 42447, Torquay, Newton Abbot (Torquay), Killed in Action, Western Front, 15/4/1918, 2nd Hampshire, 20, Kaiserschlacht (Georgette), Y

Herbert George Braund, Private, 28892, Torquay, Kingskerswell (Torquay), Died of Wounds, Home, 5/1/1918, 7th Duke of Cornwall's Light Infantry, 28, N

Fred Brearley, Private, 84863, Littlewood, Blackpool (Torquay), Died of Wounds (Gas), Home, 31/8/1917, Royal Army Medical Corps, 37, Western Front, N

Frederick Bridgman, Private, 2962, Torquay, Exeter (Torquay), Killed in Action, Western Front, 13/11/1916, 17th Royal Fusiliers, Unknown, Battle of the Somme, Y

William Louis Bridgman, 2nd Lieutenant, N/A, Torquay, Unknown (Torquay), Died of Wounds, Western Front, 20/9/1917, 6th Royal Fusiliers, 27, Battle of Passchendaele, Y

Thomas Brimblecombe, Private, G/1133, Torquay, Croydon, Surrey (Putney Hill), Died of Wounds, Western Front, 13/8/1915, 7th West Surrey, Unknown, Western Front, N

Sydney James Brimicombe, Sergeant, 8200, Staverton, Torquay, Killed in Action, Western Front, 16/9/1916, 2nd Coldstream Guards, 25, Battle of the Somme, Y

Ernest Samuel Brown, Private, 30035, Torquay, Torquay, Killed in Action, Western Front, 28/4/1917, 8th Somerset Light Infantry, 36, Battle of Arras, Y

Stanley William Bryant, Private, 102056, Plymouth, Newton Abbot (Torquay), Killed in Action, Western Front, 14/4/1918, Labour Corps, Unknown, *Kaiserschlacht*, N

Walter Ernest Bunclark, Sergeant, 16/622, Torquay, Bradford (Unknown), Killed in Action, Western Front, 27/2/1917, 16th West Yorkshire, 19, Western Front, N

John Burke, Corporal, R/854, Torquay, Porth (Torquay), Killed in Action, Western Front, 30/11/1917, 10th King's Royal Rifle Corps, Unknown, Battle of Cambrai, Y

Harold Bush, Lance Corporal, SPTS/4519, Devonport, Newton Abbot (Torquay), Died of Wounds, Western Front, 11/5/1917, 23rd Royal Fusiliers, 32, Western Front, Y

Stewart Caig, Sapper, 510339, Torquay, Exeter (Torquay), Killed in Action, Western Front, 13/5/1917, Royal Engineers, 58th Signal Company, 33, Battle of Arras, Y

William James Came, Lieutenant Corporal, 2262, Torquay, Pontypridd (Unknown), Killed in Action, Gallipoli, 17/8/1915, 1/5th Welsh, 27, Gallipoli, Y

Frederick George Cameron, Private, 58003, Torquay, London, Died of Wounds, Western Front, 11/4/1917, 17th King's Liverpool, 19, Western Front, Y

Harry James Campbell, Corporal, 510356, Torquay, Torquay, Died of Wounds, Western Front, 25/10/1917, Royal Engineers, 58th Signal Company, Unknown, Battle of Passchendaele, Y

George Carpenter, Private, 267825, Torquay, Abergavenny (Torquay), Killed in Action, Western Front, 12/4/1918, 2nd Monmouthshire, 27, Kaiserschlacht (Georgette), Y (as F.G.)

Robert William Carter, Gunner, 965914, Torquay, London (Unknown), Died of Wounds, Western Front, 27/7/1917, Royal Field Artillery, 235th Brigade, 25, Western Front (Near Ypres), N

William Matthews Paul Cater, Private, 20567, Torquay, Newton Abbot (Unknown), Killed in Action, Western Front, 18/6/1918, 6th Dorset, 18, Kaiserschlacht, N

James Arthur Leslie Chambers, Rifleman, 391191, Torquay, Unknown, Died of Wounds, Western Front, 4/5/1917, 9th London (Queen Victoria's Rifles), 26, Battle of Arras, N

Thomas James Chapman, Private, 23828, Torquay, Cardiff (Torquay), Killed in Action, Western Front, 10/7/1916, 14th Welsh, Unknown, Battle of the Somme, N

Alfred James Chapple, Private, 8793, Torquay, Birmingham, Killed in Action, Western Front, 7/11/1915, 11th Royal Warwickshire, Unknown, Western Front, N

David Ching, Corporal, 91992, Torquay, Ammanford (Pantyffynon), Killed in Action, Western Front, 28/9/1918, Royal Engineers, 225th Tunnelling Company, 18, Hundred Days, Y

Leonard Bowden, Chudleigh, Private, 4433, Newton Abbot (Torquay), Killed in Action, Western Front, 14/10/1917, Machine Gun Corps, 29, Battle of Passchendaele, Y

Reginald Cocks, Sergeant, G/52607, Torquay, Exeter (Torquay), Killed in Action, Western Front, 30/11/1917, 17th Royal Fusiliers, 24, Battle of Cambrai, Y

Terence Michael Phillip Coffey, Private, 32688, Torquay, Newton Abbot (Torquay), Killed in Action, Western Front, 15/9/1916, 5th Oxford and Bucks Light Infantry, 19, Battle of the Somme, Y

Archibald Lawrence Cole, Private, STK/1417, Torquay, London, Killed in Action, Western Front, 23/4/1917, 10th Royal Fusiliers, 26, Battle of Arras, N

George Henry Cole, Private, 34342, Torquay, Wokingham (Unknown), Died, Italy, 6/11/1918, 2nd Warwickshire, 22, N

John Cook, Private, 29799, Ashburton, Exeter (Torquay), Died of Wounds, Western Front, 26/9/1918, 10th King's Shropshire Light Infantry, Unknown, Hundred Days, Y

Percy Reginald Coplestone, Private, 3318, Torquay, Exeter (Paignton), Died, Home, 17/11/1915, Royal Gloucestershire Hussars (aka Gloucestershire Yeomanry), Unknown, N

Percy Edgar Coppen, Private, 30042, London, Torquay, Died of Wounds, Western Front, 16/9/1917, 8th Somerset Light Infantry, 23, Western Front, Y

Reginald Charles Perring Edwards, Private, S/201477, Brixham, London (Torquay), Killed in Action, Western Front, 30/10/1917, 1st/28th Bn. London (Artists' Rifles), 24, Battle of Passchendaele, Y

Percy Symons Cornish, Private, 633382, Barnstaple, Torquay, Killed in Action, Western Front, 1/10/1916, 1/20th (Blackheath and Woolwich) Londons, Unknown, Battle of the Somme, Y

Walter Coyte, Acting Sergeant, 416157, Modbury, London (Torquay), Died of Wounds,

Western Front, 19/3/1918, Chinese Labour Corps, 60th Company, Unknown, Western Front (Near Ypres), N

Frederick Gabriel Cribbett, Gunner, 48609, Torquay, Torquay, Died of Wounds, Western Front, 22/8/1916, Royal Field Artillery, 22nd Brigade, 105th Battery, 27, Battle of the Somme, Y

Charles Lewis Crocker, Sapper, 164794, Torquay, Hastings (Dartmouth), Died of Wounds, Western Front, 29/5/1918, Royal Engineers, Unknown, Kaiserschlacht, N

George Henry Croot, Private, 12604, Stoke-in-Teignhead, Exeter (Torquay), Died of Wounds, Western Front, 14/5/1916, Coldstream Guards, 22, Western Front (Near Ypres), Y

James Henry Crute, Lance Corporal, 34688, Nottingham, Torquay, Killed in Action, Western Front, 6/8/1917, 9th Loyal North Lancashire, 30, Battle of Passchendaele, Y

Herbert Ernest Dalby, Major, N/A, Unknown, Unknown (Torquay), Killed in Action, Mesopotamia, 14/10/1917, Royal Army Medical Corps, Unknown, Mesopotamian Campaign, Y

Herbert Henry Davey, Lieutenant Corporal, 1702, Torquay, Woldingham (Plymouth), Killed in Action, Western Front, 1/7/1916, 16th Middlesex, 22, Battle of the Somme, Y (as W. H.)

Stanley Davey, Rifleman, Z/2386, Torquay, Porth (Torquay), Killed in Action, Western Front, 4/5/1915, 4th Rifle Brigade, Unknown, 2nd Ypres, Y

George Davies, Driver, 11218, Cardiff, Devonport (Torquay), Died of Wounds, Western Front, 25/10/1917, Royal Field Artillery, 4th Division Ammunition Column, 35, Battle of Passchendaele, Y

Arthur Mark Dodd, Sapper, 41131, Brixham, Unknown (Torquay), Died, Home, 3/12/1917, Royal Engineers, 3rd Bridging Train, 28, Y

John Thomas Dolan, Sergeant, 3106, Torquay, Exeter (Plymouth), Died, Home, 2/2/1917, Royal Garrison Artillery, Unknown, N

Arthur Ernest Dommett, Private, 30017, London, Torquay, Killed in Action, Western Front, 30/11/1917, 7th Somerset Light Infantry, Unknown, Battle of Cambrai, Y (as A. E.)

James Down, Private, M2/033011, Torquay, London (Torquay), Killed in Action, Western Front, 25/9/1915, Royal Army Service Corps, Mounted Transport Section, 7th Field Ambulance, Unknown, Western Front (Near Ypres), Y

Alfred Downey, Trooper, 3593, Torquay, Exeter (Unknown), Killed in Action, Western Front, 26/1/1916, 1st Life Guards, Unknown, Western Front, Y

Frederick John Dustan, Rifleman, A/202307, Torquay, London, Died of Wounds, Western Front, 24/3/1918, 17th King's Royal Rifle Corps, Unknown, Kaiserschlacht (Michael), N

George Frederick Easterbrook, Private, 241984, Torquay, Torquay, Killed in Action, Western Front, 9/10/1917, 2/8th Worcestershire, Unknown, Battle of Passchendaele, Y (as Esterbrook)

Arthur Eddy, Private, 5793, Torquay, Exeter (Torquay), Killed in Action, Western Front, 13/5/1915, 19th Hussars, 23, 2nd Ypres, Y

Eric Lea Priestley Edwards, Captain, N/A, Scarborough, Unknown (Torquay), Killed in Action, Western Front, 20/9/1914, 1st East Yorkshire, 37, 1914, Y

Leonard Tarring Elliott, Private, 2131, Unknown, Larkhill (Torquay), Died, Home, 28/3/1917, Royal Army Medical Corps, Unknown, Y

Leonard Wilfred Elliott, Private, 35406, Torquay, Newton Abbot (Torquay), Killed in Action, Western Front, 16/8/1917, 7th Duke of Cornwall's Light Infantry, 20, Battle of Passchendaele, Y

Henry John Evens, Private, 166114, Torquay, Exeter (Torquay), Died, Home, 3/5/1918, 2/1st North Somerset Yeomanry, 27, Y (as Evens)

Cecil Herbert Facey, Guardsman, 9482, Torquay, Exeter (Witheridge), Killed in Action, Western Front, 6/11/1914, Coldstream Guards, 19, 1914, N

Percival Robert Farleigh, Private, 66551, Torquay, Exeter (Torquay), Killed in Action, Western Front, 30/11/1917, Royal Army Medical Corps, 101st Field Ambulance, 21, Western Front (Near Ypres), Y

John Walter Fitze Gunn, Private, G/23700, Torquay, Torquay, Killed in Action, Western Front, 4/10/1917, 1st The Queen's Own Royal West Kent, 27, Battle of Passchendaele, Y (as W J.F.)

Henry Arthur Fitzherbert, Private, 37663, East Molesley, Newton Abbot (Torquay), Died of Wounds, Western Front, 8/10/1917, 4th Worcestershire Regiment, 23, Battle of Passchendaele, Y

Gilbert John Milner Flemyng, Private, 34683, Unknown, Exeter (Torquay), At Sea, Western Front, 15/6/1917, Somerset Light Infantry, 1st Garrison Battalion, Unknown, Y

William Alfred Fragall, Sapper, 514680, Torquay, Torquay, Accidently Killed, Western Front, 27/8/1918, Royal Engineers, 567th Army Troops Company, 27, Hundred Days, Y

Frank Edward French, Private, 27106, Torquay, Newton Abbot (Torquay), Killed in Action, Western Front, 30/11/1917, 7th Somerset Light Infantry, 25, Battle of Cambrai, Y

Frank Frost, Private, 107338, Torquay, Exeter (Torquay), Died, Western Front, 3/3/1918Machine Gun Corps, 55th Battalion, 23, Western Front, N

Henry Foweraker, Private, 202713, Torquay, Woolwich (Plumstead), Killed in Action, Western Front, 27/9/1917, 2/4th Leicester, Unknown, Battle of Passchendaele, Y

William Albert Gale, Private, 25492, Torquay, London, Killed in Action, Western Front, 30/7/1916, 18th Lancashire Fusiliers, 19, Battle of the Somme, N

Ernest Garnet Gay, Private, 242036, Unknown, Torquay, Killed in Action, Western Front, 27/8/1917, 2/8th Worcestershire, Unknown, Battle of Passchendaele, Y

T.B. Getsom, Battery Quartermaster Sergeant, 89432, Unknown, Unknown (Torquay), Died, Home, 22/10/1917, Royal Field Artillery, 69th Howitzer Battery, Unknown, Y

John Gill, Lance Corporal, 16886, Torquay, Cheshunt (Torquay), Killed in Action, Western Front, 9/10/1916, 11th Essex, Unknown, Battle of the Somme, N

John Henry Gilpin, Lance Bombardier, 42924, Torquay, Caerphilly (Unknown), Killed in Action, Western Front, 6/5/1918, Royal Garrison Artillery, 122nd Heavy Battery, 28, Kaiserschlacht, N

William Henry Glanfield, Gunner, 86923, Unknown, Exeter (Torquay), Killed in

Action, Western Front, 5/8/1917, Royal Field Artillery, 72nd Battery, Unknown, Battle of Passchendaele, Y

George Gooding, Private, 72169, Torquay, Newton Abbot (Unknown), Killed in Action, Western Front, 31/5/1918, 9th Cheshire, 19, Kaiserschlacht, Y

Walter George Goss, Private, 29744, Cambridge, Totnes (Torquay), Died of Wounds, Western Front, 19/5/1917, Machine Gun Corps, 152nd Company, 19, Western Front, Y

Percival Dimmock Griffin, Gunner, 875, Mildenhall Paignton (Torquay), Died, India, 12/5/1915, Royal Field Artillery, 4th Wessex Brigade, 1/2nd Devon Battery, Unknown, Y

Henry Noel Grist, 2nd Lieutenant, N/A, Torquay, Unknown, Killed in Action, Western Front, 27/5/1917, Royal Engineers, 173rd Tunnelling Company, 31, Western Front (Near Ypres), Y

Leonard Groves, Private, 533376, Torquay, London, Killed in Action, Western Front, 24/7/1917 1/15th London, Unknown, Western Front (Near Ypres), N

Herbert George Hamblen Private, M2/073617, Guernsey, London (Torquay), Killed in Action, Western Front, 25/9/1915, Royal Army Service Corps, 21st Anti-Aircraft Section, Unknown, Battle of Loos, Y

Walter Henry Hamer, Lance Corporal, G/36815, Torquay, London (Tynemouth), Killed in Action, Western Front, 22/5/1917, 2nd Royal Fusiliers, 37, Battle of Arras, N

Reginald George Hannaford, Private, S4/143835, Torquay, Torquay, Died, Egypt, 23/2/1916, Royal Army Service Corps, 32nd Division Train, 22, Y

Percy Charles Harding, Sergeant, 9738, Torquay, London, Died of Wounds, Western Front, 6/12/1916, Royal Garrison Artillery, 30, Western Front, N

Frederick Austin Harsant, Private, 202202, Torquay, Exeter (Torquay), Died of Wounds (P.O.W), Western Front, 13/4/1918, 10th Worcestershire, 32, Y (as A. F.)

Percy William Hatton, Private, 66662, Torquay, Exeter (Brixham), Killed in Action, Western Front, 24/3/1918, Royal Army Medical Corps, 140th Field Ambulance, 26, Kaiserschlacht (Michael), N

Robert Hawkins, Pioneer, 110271, Torquay, London (Torquay), Killed in Action, Western Front, 9/11/1916, Royal Engineers, 1st Labour Battalion, 56, Battle of the Somme, Y

Frederick Ernest Hayes, Private, 50393, Torquay, Newton Abbot (Torquay), Killed in Action, Western Front, 24/10/1918, 2/6th Warwickshire, 20, Hundred Days, Y (as E.F.)

George Hayter, Private, 203132, Torquay, London (Torquay), Killed in Action, Western Front, 16/8/1917, ? Londons, 32, Battle of Passchendaele, Y

James Hayter, Private, 31588, Torquay, Exeter (Torquay), Killed in Action, Western Front, 10/10/1918, 6th Dorsets, 29, Hundred Days, Y

George Henry Heard, Sapper, 86948, Torquay, Exeter (Torquay), Killed in Action, Western Front, 21/4/1918, Royal Engineers, 171st Tunnelling Company, 42, Kaiserschlacht, Y

William Heathfield, Sapper, 43848, Torquay, Exeter (Torquay), Killed in Action, Western Front, 14/11/1916, Royal Engineers, 226th Field Company, Unknown, Battle of the Somme, Y

Albert George Henley, Gunner, 126503, Torquay, Torquay, Killed in Action, Western

Front, 18/4/1918, Royal Garrison Artillery, 154th Siege Battery, 30, Kaiserschlacht (Georgette), Y

George Hill, Shoeing Smith, 66987, Torquay, Liverpool (Unknown), Died, Western Front, 31/1/1917, Royal Field Artillery, 110th Brigade HQ, 37, Western Front, N

Percy Hill, Driver, 57394, Torquay, Warrington (Unknown), Died, Mesopotamia, 5/3/1917, Royal Field Artillery, 82nd Brigade, Unknown, Mesopotamian Campaign, N

Victor Thomas Hill, Bombardier, 109087, Torquay, London (Torquay), Killed in Action, Western Front, 19/10/1917, Royal Garrison Artillery, 19th Heavy Battery, 20, Battle of Passchendaele, Y

Raymond James Hodge, Private, 54966, Yealmpton, Torquay (Unknown), Killed in Action, Western Front, 9/4/1917, Machine Gun Corps, 193rd Company, Unknown, Battle of Arras, Y

W.J. Holman, Private, 50857, Torquay, Unknown, Died, Syria, 29/3/1918, Imperial Camel Corps, 22, Syrian Campaign, Y

Lewis Hoopern, Acting Sergeant, 41765, Torquay, Torquay, Killed in Action, Western Front, 16/5/1918, Royal Field Artillery, 150th Brigade, Unknown, Kaiserschlacht, N

Eric Horton, Lance Corporal, 7680, Unknown, London (Torquay), Killed in Action, Italy, 28/10/1918, 2nd Honourable Artillery Company, 20, Italian Front, Y

John Hornbrook, Corporal, 865255, Torquay, Torquay, Died, India, 15/6/1918, Royal Field Artillery, 1093rd Battery, 45, Y

Charles John Joseph Howard, Private, 360117, Torquay, Exeter (Torquay), Died of Wounds, Western Front, 3/5/1918, 10th King's Liverpool, 20, Kaiserschlacht, Y

Roy Humphreys, Lieutenant, N/A, Unknown, Unknown (Torquay), Killed in Action, Western Front, 4/9/1918, Royal Army Service Corps, Unknown, Hundred Days, N

Herbert William Humphries, Rifleman, 43933, Torquay, London, Killed in Action, Western Front, 24/8/1918, 18th King's Royal Rifle Corps, 27, Hundred Days, N

Harold Hunt, Private, 132494, Unknown, Exeter (Torquay), Died of Wounds, Western Front, 22/4/1918, Machine Gun Corps, 31st Battalion, Unknown, Western Front, Y (as T. H)

Harold Edward Hussey, 2nd Lieutenant, N/A, Unknown, Unknown (Torquay), Killed in Action, Mesopotamia, 25/3/1917, 1st Manchester, Unknown, Mesopotamian Campaign, Y

Francis Stephen Huxham, Private, 204212, Dartmouth, Exeter (Torquay), Killed in Action, Western Front, 22/3/1918, 7th Somerset Light Infantry, 27, Kaiserschlacht (Michael), Y

H.J. Hyde, Private, 72189, Torquay, London, Died of Wounds, Western Front, 13/11/1917, 11th Sherwood Foresters, Unknown, Battle of Passchendaele, N

Leonard Lawrence Jefford, Private, 44265, Plymouth, Newton Abbot (Torquay), Killed in Action, Western Front, 30/4/1918, 2/4th Royal Berkshire, Unknown, Kaiserschlacht, N

William Edward Jenkins, Private, 29966, Unknown, Torquay, Died of Wounds, Western Front, 11/3/1918, 8th Somerset Light Infantry, Unknown, Western Front (Near Ypres), Y

Philip Joint, Driver, 53305, Torquay, Exeter (Torquay), Died, India, 28/2/1917, Royal

Engineers, Unknown, Y

William Arthur Jones, Private, 3/3758, Torquay, Exeter (Unknown), Killed in Action, Western Front, 1/7/1916, 1st Hampshire, Unknown, Battle of the Somme, N

Albert Jordon, Sapper, 514779, Unknown, Torquay, At Sea, Egypt, 30/12/1917, Royal Engineers, 569th (Devon) Army Troops Company, Unknown, Y (as Jordan)

Sidney George Jordan, Private, 27049, Torquay, Devonport (Plymouth), Killed in Action, Western Front, 16/8/1917, 7th Somerset Light Infantry, Unknown, Battle of Passchendaele, N

Arthur Kellitt, Private, S4/145081, Torquay, Newton Abbot (Torquay), Died, Home, 2/12/1916, Royal Army Service Corps, 330th Depot Unit of Supply, Unknown, Y (as Kellett)

Edwin Gerald Kelly, Private, 204253, Paignton, Newton Abbot (Torquay), Killed in Action, Western Front, 30/11/1917, 7th Somerset Light Infantry, Unknown, Battle of Cambrai, Y

Harold Arthur Kentfield, Private, 204448, Torquay, Barnet (Unknown), Killed in Action, Western Front, 15/2/1918, 2/6th South Staffordshire, 23, Western Front, N

Jack Montague King, Private, SP/2954, Torquay, Exeter (Torquay), Killed in Action, Western Front, 31/7/1916, 24th Royal Fusiliers (City of London), Unknown, Battle of the Somme, Y

William Henry Kingcome Angel, Private, 39784, Plymouth, Reading (Torquay), Died of Wounds, Western Front, 17/6/1917, 3rd Worcestershire, 22, Western Front (Near Ypres), Y

E. Knapman, Private, 27113, Unknown, Unknown (Torquay), Died, Home, 20/8/1917, Somerset Light Infantry, Unknown, Y

William Knight, Private, M2/121523, Torquay, London (Cheltenham), Died, Palestine, 9/11/1918, Royal Army Service Corps, 956th Mechanical Transport Company, 35, Palestine Campaign, N

Charlie Alfred Richardson Labdon, Bombardier, 34427, Torquay, Bristol (Torquay), Died of Wounds, Western Front, 15/2/1917, Royal Garrison Artillery, 123rd Heavy Battery, 24, Western Front (Near Ypres), Y

Frederick Lane, Private, 3/4327, Torquay, Winchester (Portsmouth), Killed in Action, Western Front, 12/12/1914, 1st Hampshire, Unknown, 1914, N

William Gilbert Lane, Sapper, 496428, Torquay, Bristol (Unknown), Killed in Action, Western Front, 26/4/1918, Royal Engineers, 69th Field Company 22, Kaiserschlacht, N

William Henry Lang, Corporal, 514214, Torquay, Torquay, Died, Egypt, 29/5/1918, Royal Engineers, 570th Devon Works Company, 38, Y

Arthur Lavers, Private, 63273, Torquay, Torquay, Killed in Action, Western Front, 21/3/1918, Machine Gun Corps, 36th Battery, Unknown, Kaiserschlacht (Michael), N

Robert Charles Carnell Lawrence, Private, 59568, Torquay, Exeter (Torquay), Died, Home, 19/10/1918, 5th Royal Warwickshire, 18, Y

Frederick Henry Lear, Private, 36177, Torquay, Torquay, Killed in Action, Western Front, 22/3/1918, 7th Leicestershire, 21, Kaiserschlacht (Michael), Y

Sydney Paul Lewin, Lance Corporal, R/29358, Melton Mowbray, Croydon (Torquay), Died, Home, 5/8/1917, 11th King's Royal Rifle Corps, 32, N

Leonard William Lewis, Private, 66527, Torquay, Exeter (Torquay), Killed in Action, Western Front, 1/11/1916, Royal Army Medical Corps, 99th Field Ambulance, 21, Battle of the Somme, Y

F. Lightwood, Private, 9103, Kettering, Northampton (Torquay), Killed in Action, Western Front, 25/10/1916, 2nd Northamptonshire, Unknown, Battle of the Somme, Y

Cuthbert Hugh Lovett, Private, 40333, Brecon, Newton Abbot (Torquay), Killed in Action, Western Front, 14/4/1918, 1st Somerset Light Infantry, Unknown, Kaiserschlacht (Georgette), Y

Alfred Luxmore, Private, 29008, Halwill, Exeter (Torquay), Died of Wounds, Western Front, 29/5/1918, 2/4th Loyal North Lancashire, Unknown, Kaiserschlacht, Y (as Luxmoore)

Charles Herbert Mallock, Major, N/A, Torquay, Unknown (Torquay), Died of Wounds, Western Front, 5/11/1917, Royal Field Artillery, 23rd Army Brigade, 39, Battle of Passchendaele, Y

Maurice L. Mann, Private, 13796, Torquay, Exeter (Tavistock), Killed in Action, Western Front, 14/4/1917, 1st Dorset, Unknown, Western Front, N

Thomas John Charles Manning, Bombardier, 132738, Torquay, St Ives (Bath), Died of Wounds, Western Front, 29/7/1918, Royal Garrison Artillery, 32nd Siege Battery, 25, Hundred Days, N

Charles Mansfield, Sergeant, 13378, Unknown, Unknown (Torquay), Killed in Action, East Africa, 21/8/1916, 25th Royal Fusiliers (Legion of Frontiersmen), 37, East Africa Campaign, Y

E.G. Matthews, Private, 49778, Torquay, Unknown (Torquay), Died, Western Front, 24/4/1918, 2nd Northamptonshire, 19, Kaiserschlacht, Y

Edward Medland, Driver, 226560, Torquay, Devonport (Torquay), Died, Mesopotamia, 26/11/1917, Royal Field Artillery, 28th Battery, Unknown, Mesopotamian Campaign, N

Alec Walter Gerald Mercer, Private, T/242044, Torquay, Torquay (Paignton), Killed in Action, Western Front, 21/11/1917, 1st East Kent, Unknown, Battle of Cambrai, N

Ernest Miller, Private, 34662, Torquay, Porth (Unknown), Died, Western Front, 31/8/1918, 2nd Welsh, 33, Hundred Days, Y

Stanley William Henry Milton, Sergeant, 150497, Brixton, Newton Abbot (Torquay), Died, Home, 6/11/1917, Royal Engineers, Mechanical Section - Inland Waterways and Docks, 32, Y

John Henry Mitchell, Corporal, 62053, Torquay, London (Torquay), Died, Home, 5/11/1918, 15th Worcestershire, 34, Y

Walter Soper Mitchell, Private, O/1222, Torquay, Paignton (Unknown), Died, Home, 17/2/1916, Royal Army Ordnance Corps, 67th Company, 37, N

Stanley Moase, Private, 29469, Torquay, Newton Abbot (Torquay), Killed in Action, Western Front, 6/11/1917, 1st Duke of Cornwall's Light Infantry, Unknown, Battle of Passchendaele, Y

Reginald Mortimer, Private, G/52045, Torquay, Axminster (Seaton), Died of Wounds, Western Front, 1/3/1918, 24th Royal Fusiliers (City of London), 29, Western Front, N

George Henry Moses, Lance Corporal, 40014, Torquay, Wolverhampton, Killed in Action, Western Front, 18/11/1916, 10th Worcestershire, 28, Battle of the Somme, N

William Henry Moss, Private, T4/124252, Torquay, Torquay, Died, Home, 16/3/1916, Royal Army Service Corps, 274th Mechanical Transport Company, Unknown, N

John Mudge, Private, 15719, Torquay, Exeter (Torquay), Killed in Action, Western Front, 18/6/1916, 1st Coldstream Guards, 35, Western Front (Near Ypres), Y

Charles Frederick Newcombe, Private, 33659, Torquay, London (Unknown), Died of Wounds, Western Front, 21/7/1917, 7th Loyal North Lancashire, Unknown, Western Front (Near Ypres), N

Stanley John Newcombe, Private, 37843, Torquay, London (Unknown), Died of Wounds, Western Front, 16/8/1917, 2nd Royal Berkshire, Unknown, Battle of Passchendaele, N

Frederick Keith Nickels, Private, 26614, London, Hilsea (Torquay), Killed in Action, Western Front, 18/10/1916, 2nd Wiltshire, 20, Battle of the Somme, Y

Wilfred Lavis Northam, Rifleman, O/307, Torquay, London, Killed in Action, Western Front, 23/3/1918, 8th Rifle Brigade, Unknown, Kaiserschlacht, N

Alfred Northey, Lieutenant, N/A, Torquay, Unknown, Killed in Action, Western Front, 12/10/1914, 3rd Worcestershire, 28, 1914, Y

Ernest William Oldrey, Sapper, 515083, Torquay, Torquay, Killed in Action, Western Front, 28/5/1917, Royal Engineers, 567th Army Troops Company, 34, Western Front (Near Ypres), Y

Alfred Charles Oliver, Private, 11210, Torquay, Exeter (West Bay), Killed in Action, Western Front, 22/12/1914, 1st Coldstream Guards, 22, 1914, N

Charles Herbert Pack, Corporal, S/12121, Torquay, Newcastle (Torquay), Died of Wounds, Western Front, 24/8/1916, 14th Argyll and Sutherland Highlanders, 24, Battle of the Somme, Y

Lawrence Charles Walter Palk, Lieutenant Colonel, N/A, Exeter, Unknown (London), Killed in Action, Western Front, 1/7/1916, 1st Hampshire, 45, Battle of the Somme, N

Frank Wilton Palmer, Private, 241326, Torquay, Torquay, Died of Wounds, Western Front, 27/4/1918, 7th The Queen's Own Royal West Kent, 24, Kaiserschlacht, Y

William Palmer, Private, 10032, Torquay, Exeter (Torquay), Killed in Action, Western Front, 9/8/1918, 4th Dragoon Guards (Royal Irish), 24, Hundred Days, Y (as A. W.)

Howard Montague Robert Parkins, Private, 20803, Torquay, Plymouth (Unknown), Killed in Action, Western Front, 8/6/1916, 14th Gloucestershire, Unknown, Western Front, Y (as Parkin)

Ralph Stuart Payton, Lieutenant, N/A, Birmingham, Unknown (Torquay), Killed in Action, Western Front, 22/7/1916, 14th Royal Warwickshire, 22, Battle of the Somme, Y

George Edwin Pearce, Driver, 29979, Torquay, Exeter (Torquay), Died, Western Front, 30/10/1918, Royal Engineers, 33rd Division Signal Company, 28, Hundred Days, N

Charles William Peckham, Private, G/8556, Barkham, Newmarket (Torquay), Died of Wounds, Home, 11/7/1918, 7th Royal Sussex, 25, Y

Freddie Pedler, Corporal, 3972, Torquay, Bath (Larkhall), Died, Mesopotamia, 3/7/1916, 1/4th Somerset Light Infantry, 38, Mesopotamian Campaign, Y

Ernest John Perring, Rifleman, 5745, Torquay, Exeter (Torquay), Killed in Action, Western Front, 15/9/1916, 1/21st London (1st Surrey Rifles), 20, Battle of the Somme, Y

George Charles Perring, Acting Sergeant, 48210, Torquay, Torquay, Killed in Action,

Western Front, 8/7/1918, 14th Royal Warwickshire, 25, Western Front, Y

Samuel Perring, Driver, T/425719,Torquay, Exeter (Dartmouth), Died, Home, 26/10/1918, Royal Army Service Corps, 47, N/A, N

Albert Perryman, Lance Corporal, 21343, Torquay, Bath (Unknown), Killed in Action, Western Front, 24/8/1916, 1st Somerset Light Infantry, 23, Western Front (Near Ypres), N

Alfred Pethick, Gunner, 87283, Torquay, London (Unknown), Died of Wounds, Western Front, 12/4/1917, Royal Field Artillery, 63rd Brigade, Unknown, Western Front, N

Charles Samuel Phillips, Private, 202342, Torquay, Penzance (Unknown), Killed in Action, Western Front, 30/11/1917, 7th Duke of Cornwall's Light Infantry, Unknown, Battle of Cambrai, N

Robert John Phillips, Private, 46296, Torquay, Torquay, Killed in Action, Western Front, 22/4/1918, 19th Lancashire Fusiliers, 31, Kaiserschlacht (Georgette), Y

Walter Phillips, Private, 18871, Torquay, Portsmouth (Plymouth), Killed in Action, Western Front, 15/9/1916, 15th Hampshire, Unknown, Battle of the Somme, N

Bert Pitt, Private, 33868, Exeter, Torquay, Killed in Action, Western Front, 28/4/1917, 10th Loyal North Lancashire, 21, Battle of Arras, Y

George Henry Pitts, Driver, 740938, Torquay, Newport (Unknown), Died, Home, 1/6/1918, Royal Field Artillery, 65th Division Ammunition Column, 27, Y

Ernest Pleace, Private, 88467, Torquay, Torquay, Killed in Action, Western Front, 24/12/1917, 7th King's Liverpool, Unknown, Western Front (Near Ypres), Y

Charles Henry Poat, Gunner, 10086, Torquay, Nuneaton (Unknown), Died of Wounds, Western Front, 11/5/1917, Royal Field Artillery, 123rd Brigade, 28, Western Front, N

Percy Pomroy, Lance Corporal, 11963, Torquay, Mill Hill (Hornsey Vale), Killed in Action, Western Front, 8/1/1917, 13th Middlesex, Unknown, Western Front, N

Leonard John Poplett, Rifleman, 555058, Torquay, London, At Sea, Egypt, 30/12/1917, 1/16th (Queens Westminster Rifles) Londons, 19, At Sea, N

Thomas Ladas Powers, Private, 3139, Stratford-Upon-Avon, Unknown (Torquay), Died, Home, 26/2/1915, 24th Royal Fusiliers, 20, Y

Charles Lacey Priestley, Captain, N/A, Torquay, Unknown (Torquay), Died of Wounds, Western Front, 11/11/1917, 1st Gloucester, 20, Battle of Passchendaele, Y

Henry Puckett, Private, 267586, Torquay, London (Unknown), Died of Wounds, Western Front, 19/4/1917, 1st Oxford and Bucks Light Infantry, Unknown, Western Front, N

Edmund Charles Pugsley, Private, 28996, Torquay, Totnes (Unknown), Died, Egypt, 17/12/1917, 1/4th Duke of Cornwall's Light Infantry, 39, N

Robert Leslie Pullman, Private, 29358, Torquay, Newton Abbot (Torquay), Killed in Action, Western Front, 28/9/1918, 1st Duke of Cornwall's Light Infantry, Unknown, Hundred Days, Y

Arthur Robin Putt, Lance Sergeant, Z/2604, Torquay, Finsbury - London (Torquay), Killed in Action, Western Front, 21/3/1918, 16th Rifle Brigade, 28, Kaiserschlacht (Michael), Y

James Henry Quiller, Private, 18382, Torquay, Barnoldswick (Great Harwood), Killed in Action, Italy, 27/10/1918, 10th West Riding, Unknown, Italian Front, N

William Alfred Rendell, Private, 15066, Torquay, Exeter (Torquay), Killed in Action,

Western Front, 28/4/1917, 8th Somerset Light Infantry, 21, Battle of Arras, Y

Herbert Charles Roberts, Private, 10033, Torquay, Exeter (Southborough), Died of Wounds, Western Front, 27/3/1918, 4th Dragoon Guards (Royal Irish), 32, Kaiserschlacht (Michael), Y

Albert Percy Robins, Private, M/188271, Torquay, Plymouth, Died of Wounds, Western Front, 30/9/1917, Royal Army Service Corps, Unknown, Battle of Passchendaele, N

Henry George Gordon Rutherfurd, Private, STK/518, Hartford, London (Torquay), Killed in Action, Western Front, 15/7/1916, 10th Royal Fusiliers, 30, Battle of the Somme, Y

Herbert Sawyer, Private, 17913, Torquay, North Shields (Unknown), Killed in Action, Western Front, 26/9/1916, 8th Northumberland Fusiliers, 24, Battle of the Somme, N

James Clarence Ethelbert Scholes, Lance Corporal, 24615, Torquay, Liverpool (Torquay), Killed in Action, Western Front, 1/7/1916, 18th King's Liverpool, Unknown, Battle of the Somme, Y

H. Scott, Sapper, 515929, Torquay, Torquay, Killed in Action, Western Front, 10/4/1918, Royal Engineers, 254th Company, 21, Kaiserschlacht, Y

William George Scott, Private, 20796, Torquay, Unknown (Torquay), Killed in Action, Western Front, 24/5/1915, 14th Gloucestershire, 19, Western Front, Y

William Scragg, Bombardier, 9755, Torquay, Unknown, Died, Home, 20/3/1918, 3rd Royal Dublin Fusiliers, 40, N

Joshua Shapcott, Company Sergeant Major, 505, Torquay, Torquay, Died, Home, 18/3/1916, Royal Engineers, 2nd/1st Devon Fortress Company, 56, Y

Albert Sharland, Private, 28306, Torquay, Newton Abbot (Torquay), Killed in Action, Western Front, 23/8/1917, 6th Duke of Cornwall's Light Infantry, 32, Battle of Passchendaele, Y

William Goodwin Blake Shinner, Lieutenant, N/A, Torquay, Unknown (Torquay), Died of Wounds, Western Front, 2/1/1918, 28th London (Artists Rifles), Unknown, Western Front, N

Hugh Archie Shopland, Bombardier, 1380, Torquay, Exeter (Unknown), Died of Wounds, Western Front, 26/9/1915, Royal Field Artillery, 71st Brigade, 27, Battle of Loos, Y (as A. Shopland)

Claude Sidney Sims, Sapper, 2079, Torquay, Portsmouth (Toronto), Died, Home, 23/4/1916, Royal Engineers, 2/4th Hampshire Fortress Company, 23, Western Front, N

Charles Henry Skinner, Sapper, 139868, Plymouth, Newton Abbot (Torquay), Killed in Action, Western Front, 20/3/1917, Royal Engineers, 201st Field Company, Unknown, Western Front, Y

Albert William Smerdon, Lance Corporal, 36155, Torquay, Ashford (Unknown), Killed in Action, Western Front, 21/3/1918, 7th Leicestershire, 28, Kaiserschlacht (Michael), Y

John Smith, Private, TF/292487, Whitley, Exeter (Torquay), Killed in Action, Western Front, 20/7/1917, 3/10th Middlesex, 32, Western Front, Y

Ernest James Soper, Acting Sergeant, S/4/084853, Torquay, Exeter (Torquay), Died, Home, 17/9/1915, Royal Army Service Corps, 'A' Supply Company, 40, Y

Ernest William Southwood, Lance Corporal, 29476, Torquay, Newton Abbot (Torquay),

Died of Wounds, Western Front, 1/11/1917, 1st Duke of Cornwall's Light Infantry, Unknown, Battle of Passchendaele, Y

Herbert Wilfred Spear, Rifleman, 553661, Torquay, Newton Abbot (Brockley), Killed in Action, Western Front, 7/6/1918, 1/16th (Queens Westminster Rifles) Londons, 20, Kaiserschlacht, Y

Harold Spencer, Corporal, 1675, Torquay, Stockton-On-Tees (Middlesborough), Died, Italy, 3/11/1918, 2nd Royal Warwickshire, 32, N

Herbert Reginald Kingston Splatt, Private, 6454, Torquay, Torquay, Killed in Action, Western Front, 17/11/1914, 3rd Dragoon Guards, 21, 1914, Y

George Albert Spurr, Rifleman, R/5184, Torquay, London (Unknown), Killed in Action, Western Front, 11/8/1915, 2nd King's Royal Rifle Corps, 37, Western Front, N

Harold Squires, Private, 35911, East Allington, Newton Abbot (Torquay), Died of Wounds, Home, 11/8/1918, 1st Oxford and Bucks Light Infantry, 20, Y

Frederick George Stamp, Sapper, 146790, Torquay, Torquay, Killed in Action, Western Front, 2/12/1917, Royal Engineers, 151st Field Company, 28, Western Front, Y

Frederick Stanbury, Gunner, 30318, Torquay, London (Torquay), Died of Wounds, Western Front, 29/8/1917, Royal Garrison Artillery, 305th Siege Battery, Unknown, Battle of Passchendaele, Y

George Sydney Steed, Private, 18442, Torquay, Unknown (Torquay), Died, Western Front, 21/10/1918, 5th Grenadier Guards, 25, Hundred Days, Y

Charles Neville Carleton Stiff, Captain, N/A, Unknown, Unknown (Torquay), Killed in Action, Western Front, 22/3/1918, 4th Yorkshire, 36, Kaiserschlacht (Michael), Y

A.E. Stockman, Private, 31360, Torquay, Unknown, Killed in Action, Western Front, 24/4/1917, 16th Lancashire Fusiliers, Unknown, Western Front, Y

Edwin Stoneman, Driver, 62641, Torquay, Unknown (Torquay), Died, Western Front, 2/11/1917, Royal Field Artillery, 75th Brigade, 22, Battle of Passchendaele, Y

Sidney Richard Sweeney, Rifleman, 305766, Torquay, London (Torquay), Killed in Action, Western Front, 10/8/1918, 5th London (London Rifle Brig.), Unknown, Hundred Days, Y

William Henry Tanner, Private, 241356, Torquay, Newton Abbot (Unknown), Killed in Action, Western Front, 21/3/1918, 8th The Queen's Own Royal West Kent, 31, Kaiserschlacht (Michael), Y

Percy Tarr, Private, 4347, Torquay, Newton Abbot (Torquay), Killed in Action, Western Front, 2/7/1917, 8th Royal Fusiliers, 30, Western Front, Y

Frank Tayler, Private, 702190, Torquay, Newton Abbot (Torquay), Killed in Action, Palestine, 31/10/1917, 23rd London, 28, Palestine Campaign, Y

Henry Thomas, Acting Corporal, 140997, Torquay, Chatham (Torquay), Died of Wounds, Western Front, 13/5/1918, Royal Engineers, 5th Foreway Company, 21, Kaiserschlacht, Y

William Henry Cecil Thomas, Private, 6153, Torquay, Unknown (Torquay), Killed in Action, Western Front, 16/8/1916, 1/4th Oxford and Bucks Light Infantry, 30, Battle of the Somme, Y

Reginald Charles Tickell, Guardsman, 16629, Torquay, London (Unknown), Killed in Action, Western Front, 28/3/1918, 2nd Grenadier Guards, 19, Kaiserschlacht (Michael), Y

William Henry Tope, Private, 481940, Torquay, Newton Abbot (Torquay), Died, Home, 6/11/1918, Labour Corps, 27, Y

Ronald Claud Tozer, Private, 11410, Torquay, Wrexham (Fishguard), Killed in Action, Western Front, 13/11/1914, 2nd Royal Welsh Fusiliers, Unknown, 1914, N

Richard James Treby, Lance Corporal, 241983, Torquay, Torquay, Died (P.O.W), Western Front, 17/7/1918, 2/8th Worcestershire, 23, Y

Ernest William Truman, Sergeant, 6065, Torquay, Unknown, Killed in Action, Western Front, 10/5/1915, 4th Dragoon Guards (Royal Irish), Unknown, 2nd Ypres, N

Stanley Phillip Tucker, Private, 19819, Torquay, Newton Abbot (Torquay), Died, Western Front, 14/9/1917, 6th Dorset, 21, Western Front, Y

William Tucker, Private, SS/23349, Torquay, Unknown (Torquay), Died, Home, 21/9/1918, Royal Army Service Corps, 36, Y

John Tunkin, Driver, 81523, Torquay, Exeter (Unknown), At Sea, Salonika, 23/10/1915, Royal Field Artillery, 29th Division Ammunition Column, 20, Y

Reginald Percy Turner, Private, 38716, Torquay, Exeter (Unknown), Died, Western Front, 23/3/1918, 14th Gloucestershire, 31, Kaiserschlacht (Michael), Y

Sidney Arthur Turner, Private, 34052, Torquay, Newton Abbot (Torquay), Killed in Action, Western Front, 10/10/1917, 2nd Essex, Unknown, Battle of Passchendaele, Y

William Tyernan Procter, Rifleman, 4312, Exeter, Newton Abbot (Torquay), Died, Home, 3/7/1916, 5th London Regiment (London Rifle Brig.), Unknown, Y (as Proctor)

Claudian Stewart Tyler, Private, 36309, Bristol, Exeter (Torquay), Killed in Action, Western Front, 4/11/1918, 2nd Wiltshire, Unknown, Hundred Days, Y

William Edgar Vanstone, Rifleman, 13033, Torquay, Exeter (Torquay), Died of Wounds, Western Front, 15/9/1916, 8th King's Royal Rifle Corps, Unknown, Battle of the Somme, Y (as W.V.)

William Arthur Vincent, Private, 5500, Torquay, Torquay, Killed in Action, Western Front, 14/6/1916, 2/8th Worcestershire, 24, Western Front, Y

Frederick William Wallis, Private, 44168, Torquay, Newton Abbot (Torquay), Killed in Action, Western Front, 2/5/1918, 2/4th Royal Berkshire, 18, Kaiserschlacht, Y

William Henry Warren, Private, G/24323, Torquay, Kingston-on-Thames (Sutton), Died of Wounds, Western Front, 2/2/1917, 8th Royal West Surrey, 18, Western Front, N

Francis George Stuart Watson, 2nd Lieutenant, N/A, Stoke Gabriel, Unknown (Torquay), Killed in Action, Western Front, 23/10/1916, 2nd Lancashire Fusiliers, 19, Battle of the Somme, Y

John Cornish Watson, Sapper, 514667, Unknown, Torquay, At Sea, Egypt, 30/12/1917, Royal Engineers, 567th Army Troops Company, 35, Y

William Ben Watson, Sergeant, 463008, Unknown, Exeter (Torquay), Killed in Action, Western Front, 30/5/1918, Royal Army Medical Corps, 46th (Wessex) Casualty Clearing Station, 49, Kaiserschlacht, Y

John William Way, Private, TR/8/17734, Torquay, Newton Abbot (Torquay), Died, Home, 28/6/1917, 16th Gloucestershire, 18, Y

Archibald Henry Waymouth, Private, 81573, Torquay, Abertillery (Unknown), Killed in Action, Western Front, 11/4/1918, 1/8th Durham Light Infantry, Unknown, Kaiserschlacht (Georgette), Y

George Alfred Waymouth, Gunner, 967, Torquay, Paignton (Unknown), Died, India, 4/9/1915, Royal Field Artillery, 4th Wessex Brigade, 1/2nd Devon Battery, Unknown, N

Dennis Henry Webb, Lieutenant, N/A, Unknown, Unknown (Torquay), Killed in Action, Western Front, 10/11/1917, Machine Gun Corps, Unknown, Battle of Passchendaele, Y

Edward Courtenay Webber, Guardsman, 2037, Torquay, Taunton (Unknown), Died of Wounds, Western Front, 27/8/1918, 4th Guards Machine Gun Regiment, 35, Hundred Days, N

Frank Furneaux Weeks, Sergeant, Y/1732, Torquay, London (New Malden), Died of Wounds, Western Front, 10/7/1917, 2nd King's Royal Rifle Corps, 34, Western Front (Near Ypres), N

Harry Weeks, Rifleman, R/34202, Torquay, London (Paddington), Died, Western Front, 13/7/1918, 13th King's Royal Rifle Corps, 27, Kaiserschlacht, N

Frederick Harold Westcott, Lance Corporal, SP/2987, Torquay, Exeter (Torquay), Killed in Action, Western Front, 31/7/1916, 24th Royal Fusiliers, Unknown, Western Front, Y

Sidney Arthur West, Private, 29634, London, Newton Abbot (Torquay), Died (P.O.W), Western Front, 27/4/1918, 1/5th Duke of Cornwall's Light Infantry, Unknown, Y

Ernest Albert Westaway, Private, 84231, Marldon, Torquay, Killed in Action, Western Front, 8/10/1918, Machine Gun Corps, 21st Battalion, 29, Hundred Days, Y

Martin Lloyd Weston, Private, 14232, Torquay, Winchester (Littleheath), Killed in Action, Gallipoli, 10/8/1915, 10th Hampshire, 25, Gallipoli, N

Fred Wheeler, Lance Corporal, G/19495, Torquay, Sutton (Cheam), Died, Home, 2/5/1917, 1st East Kent, 35, N

Francis Joseph Whiddon, Private, 27066, Torquay, Torquay, Killed in Action, Western Front, 1/10/1916, 7th Somerset Light Infantry, 31, Battle of the Somme, Y (as Whidden)

William Henry Whiddon, Private, 12759, Torquay, Exeter (Torquay), Died of Wounds, Western Front, 17/6/1916, Coldstream Guards, Unknown, Western Front (Near Ypres), Y (as Whidden)

Herman William White, Staff Sergeant, 3004, East Portlemouth, Torquay, Died, Home, 12/2/1917, Army Ordnance Corps, 26th Special Company, 24, Y

Mark Samuel White, Private, 34794, Rattery, Newton Abbot (Torquay), Died of Illness, Western Front, 19/3/1917, Labour Corps, 41, Western Front (Near Ypres), Y

William Thomas White, Lance Corporal, 11850, Torquay, Ton-y-Pandy (Unknown), Died, Western Front, 8/5/1917, 12th Gloucestershire Regiment, 23, Battle of Arras, Y

Edward John Whiteway, W.O. Class 2, 8512, Torquay, Stratford (Unknown), Killed in Action, Western Front, 23/10/1917, 9th King's Own Yorkshire Light Infantry, Unknown, Battle of Passchendaele, Y

Ernest Arthur Williams, Sergeant, L/6973, Rangoon, Canterbury (Torquay), Killed in Action, Western Front, 15/9/1916, 1st East Kent, Unknown, Battle of the Somme, Y

Henry Williams, Private, 74560, Penzance, Newton Abbot (Torquay), Killed in Action, Western Front, 24/7/1916, Royal Army Medical Corps, 8th Field Ambulance, Unknown, Battle of the Somme, Y

Leonard Charles Williams, 2nd Lieutenant, N/A, Torquay, Unknown (Torquay), Died of Wounds, Western Front, 10/11/1917, 1st Lincolnshire, 19, Battle of Passchendaele, Y

Ralph Robinson Willott, Private, 241340, Torquay, Exeter (Newton Abbot), Killed in Action, Western Front, 23/3/1918, 10th The Queen's Own Royal West Kent, 27, Kaiserschlacht (Michael), N

Thomas George Francis Wills (known as Frank), 2nd Lieutenant, N/A, Newton - Wales, Unknown (Torquay), Killed in Action, Western Front, 2/9/1918, 3rd Somerset Light Infantry, 24, Hundred Days, Y

Percy John Wills, Sapper, 149013, Torquay, Kingston-on-Thames (Surbiton), Died, Mesopotamia, 6/11/1917, Royal Engineers, 15th Division Signal Company, 40, Mesopotamian Campaign, N

Henry Charles Windeatt, Private, 20717, Torquay, Newton Abbot (Torquay), Killed in Action, Western Front, 30/8/1916, 1/8th Worcestershire, 20, Battle of the Somme, Y

Gilbert Joseph Winget, Corporal, 609, Torquay, London (Torquay), Died of Wounds, Western Front, 1/11/1914, 12th (Prince of Wales's Royal) Lancers, 30, 1914, Y

Ernest Herbert Winter, Private, SPTS/4470, Torquay, Newton Abbot (Torquay), Died of Wounds, Western Front, 18/2/1917, 23rd Royal Fusiliers, 21, Western Front, Y

Herbert Richard Thomas Winter, 2nd Corporal, 514197, Torquay, Torquay, Killed in Action, Western Front, 27/8/1918, Royal Engineers, 567th Army Troops Company, 27, Hundred Days, Y

Alfred John Wollacott, Acting Corporal, T/240322, Torquay, Farnham, Died, India, 14/7/1918, 1/5th West Surrey, Unknown, N

Harry Woodward, Gunner, 190349, Barnet, Torquay, Killed in Action, Western Front, 16/5/1918, Royal Garrison Artillery, 122nd Siege Battery, 28, Kaiserschlacht, Y

Cecil Norman Worth, Lance Corporal, 9139, Kingsbridge, Torquay, Died of Wounds, Western Front, 2/6/1915, 3rd Hussars, 21, Western Front, Y

Thomas Richard Worth, Private, 84232, Stoke-in-Teignhead, Torquay, Killed in Action, Italy, 29/6/1918, Machine Gun Corps, 23rd Battalion, 34, Italian Front, Y

Frederick John Young, Private, 5274, Torquay, Camberwell (Peckham), Killed in Action, Western Front, 1/10/1916, 1/20th (Blackheath and Woolwich) Londons, 38, Battle of the Somme, N

Canadian Expeditionary Force

Kenneth Bell-Irving, Captain, N/A, Torquay, Canada, Died of Wounds, Western Front, 22/10/1917, 8th East Surrey, 24, Battle of Passchendaele, Y

William Blanchard Ayers, Private, 428268, Torquay, New Westminster, Killed in Action, Western Front, 19/10/1915, 7th Canadian Infantry, 34, Western Front (Near Ypres), N

Herbert Lewis Bond, Corporal, 688216, Torquay, Kamloops, Killed in Action, Western Front, 26/10/1917, 47th Canadian Infantry, 31, Battle of Passchendaele, Y

Leonard Adolphus Bond, Private, 688215, Torquay, Kamloops, Killed in Action, Western Front, 31/3/1917, 47th Canadian Infantry, 26, Western Front, Y

Albert Frank Chapman, Private, 187545, Torquay, Winnipeg, Died, Western Front, 31/8/1918, 8th Canadian Infantry, 25, Hundred Days, Y

Henry James Cliff, Corporal, 258917, Torquay, Calgary, Killed in Action, Western Front, 5/6/1917, 8th Canadian Railway Troops, 28, Western Front (Near Ypres), N

Thomas William Eric Dixon, Captain, 109309, Torquay, Toronto, Killed in Action, Western Front, 3/8/1918, 4th Canadian Mounted Rifles, 25, Western Front (Near Ypres), N

Seymour George English, Private, 159068, Torquay, Toronto, Died, Western Front, 28/5/1917, 18th Canadian Infantry, 27, Western Front, N

Frank Augustus Ridout Evans, Lance Corporal, 6224, Torquay, Valcartier, Died of Wounds, Western Front, 14/4/1916, Princess Patricia's Canadian Light Infantry, 24, Western Front (Near Ypres), N

George Follett, Private, 1432, Torquay, Valcartier, Died, Western Front, 21/6/1915, 8th Canadian Infantry, 25, Western Front, Y

Reginald Arthur Gibbs, Private, 687151, Torquay, Kamloops, British Columbia, Killed in Action, Western Front, 30/10/1917, 72nd Canadian Infantry, 20, Battle of Passchendaele, Y

Philip Thomas Godfrey, Private, 775295, Torquay, Toronto, Died, Western Front, 11/1/1917, 38th Canadian Infantry, 25, Western Front, N

David Gerard Gylde, Private, 3206367, Torquay, Calgary, Died, Western Front, 29/9/1918, 10th Canadian Infantry, 33, Hundred Days, N

Samuel Hawkins, Private, 447388, Torquay, Calgary, Died, Western Front, 26/9/1916, 14th Canadian Infantry, 27, Battle of the Somme, Y

Mark Hewett, Private, 859736, Torquay, Winnipeg, Died, Western Front, 15/11/1917, 43rd Canadian Infantry, 24, Western Front, Y

Edwin James Martin, Private, 246053, Torquay, Ottawa, Died, Western Front, 15/1/1918, 38th Canadian Infantry, 35, Western Front, N

William Mudge, Lance Corporal, 469121, Torquay, Unknown, Died, Home, 22/8/1917, 64th Canadian Infantry, 56, N

Frederick John Southcombe, Private, 2590969, Unknown, Unknown, Killed in Action, Western Front, 26/9/1918. 47th Canadian Infantry, 25, Hundred Days, Y

William George Turner, Lance Corporal, 429091, Torquay, New Westminster, Killed in Action, Western Front, 2/9/1918, 7th Battalion Canadian Infantry, 28, Hundred Days, Y

William John Vanstone, Sergeant, 16711, Torquay, Valcartier, Died, Western Front, 3/6/1916, 7th Canadian Infantry, 32, Western Front (Near Ypres), N

Australian Imperial Force

Charles Todd Crompton Chambers, Private, 156, Torquay, Perth – Western Australia, Died of Wounds, Gallipoli, 6/8/1915, 11th Battalion, Australian Imperial Force (Infantry), Unknown, Gallipoli, N

Reginald Morgan, Corporal, 2284, Torquay, Liverpool - New South Wales, Died of Wounds, Western Front, 25/11/1916, 19th Battalion, Australian Imperial Force (Infantry), 28, Western Front, N

Thomas Gurney Oliver, Lance Corporal, 2943, Torquay, Liverpool - New South Wales, Killed in Action, Western Front, 5/8/1918, 3rd Battalion, Australian Imperial Force (Infantry), 29, Western Front, Y

New Zealand Expeditionary Force

Charles Keith Grant, Private, 10/2163, Torquay, Unknown (Huntersville, New Zealand), Killed in Action, Gallipoli, 8/8/1915, 5th Wellington Infantry, 25, Gallipoli, N

Harold Henry Lane, Private, 10/3321, Torquay, Wellington, Died of Wounds, Western Front, 17/6/1916, 2nd Wellington, 30, Western Front, Y

Archer Ernest Mortimore, Sergeant, 6/1638, Unknown, Unknown (Ashburton, New Zealand), Killed in Action, Gallipoli, 13/8/1915, 2nd Canterbury Infantry, 27, Gallipoli, Y

British Indian Army

Eustace Hammick, Captain, Unknown, Torquay, N/A, Died of Wounds, Egypt, 8/10/1918, 17th Indian Infantry (Loyal Regiment), 29, Palestine Campaign, N

Wilfred Hardinge Heinig, Captain, N/A, Calcutta, India, Unknown (Torquay), Killed in Action, Mesopotamia, 6/4/1916, 54th Sikhs (Frontier Force), 28, Mesopotamian Campaign, Y

Dermot Patrick O'Shea, Lieutenant, N/A, Unknown, Unknown (Torquay), Died, Yemen, 11/9/1917, 69th Punjabis, Unknown, N/A, Y

Wilfred Bernard O'Shea, 2nd Lieutenant, N/A, Unknown, Unknown (Torquay), Died of Wounds, Mesopotamia, 23/5/1915, 1/8th Ghurkha Rifles, 20, Mesopotamian Campaign, Y

John Holberton Whitehead, Lieutenant Colonel, N/A, Torquay, Unknown, Died of Wounds, Mesopotamia, 12/1/1917, 4/93rd Burma Infantry, Unknown, Mesopotamian Campaign, Y

Royal Air Force Casualties

Frank Veron Bonyun, 2nd Lieutenant, 81142, Trinidad, West Indies, Unknown (Torquay), Killed in Action, Western Front, 02/01/1918, Royal Flying Corps, 32nd Squadron, 18, Western Front (Near Ypres). Y

H.J. Ford, Air Mechanic 1st Class, 1587, Unknown, Unknown (Torquay), Unknown, Western Front, 18/08/1918, Royal Air Force, 23, Y

William Charles Smith, 2nd Lieutenant, Unknown, Oxford, Unknown (Torquay), Unknown, Western Front, 08/02/1918, Royal Flying Corps, No.1 Squadron, 22, N/A, Y

Royston Clement Wickett, Lieutenant, Unknown, Torquay, Unknown (Torquay), Killed in Action, Western Front, 9/8/1918, Royal Air Force, 6th Squadron, 20, Western Front, Y

Royal Navy Casualties

Name/ Rank / Number / Date of Death / Ship or Regiment / Battle (if applicable) / Age at death / On Torquay War Memorial Y/N?

George Avery, Able Seaman, J/18992, 31/05/1916, *Indefatigable*, Jutland, 20, Y

Frank Babbage, Officer's Steward 3rd Class, L/4557, 31/05/1916, *Indefatigable*, Jutland, 19, Y

Geoffrey Bruce Barchard, Midshipman, Unknown, 22/09/1914, *Aboukir*, Sunk by U-9, Unknown, Y

Ernest Edward Bastard, Petty Officer, 207705, 16/09/1917, Submarine G9, Friendly Fire Incident, 32, Y

Albert Edward Beer, Petty Officer, 193877, 21/08/1917, Valla (Q Ship *Vala*), Sunk by *UB54*, 36, Y

John Bishop, Petty Officer, 185090, 14/03/1918, *Defiance*, N/A, 40, Y

Albert George Bourhill, Cook's Mate, M/12064, 31/05/1916, *Defence*, Jutland, 18, Y

Norman Bovey, Ordinary Seaman, J/43633, 09/07/1917, *Vanguard*, Explosion in dock (Scapa Flow), 18, Y

Max Albert Capron, Officer's Steward 2nd Class, L/5047, 15/07/1917, *Tarpon*, N/A, 23, Y

Thomas Chick, Stoker 1st Class, K/19218, 31/05/1916, *Defence*, Jutland, 24, Y

John Christie, 1st Class Stoker, 278341, 13/05/1915, *Goliath*, Gallipoli, 43, Y

James William Clark, Gunner, RMA/1656 (S), 26/03/1918, Royal Marine Artillery - Howitzer Brigade, Western Front (Michael), 26, Y

William Cobb, Leading Seaman, 225777, 31/05/1916, *Indefatigable*, Jutland, 27, Y

John Lashbrook Cole, Private, PLY/15634, 29/12/1915, Plymouth Battalion Royal Naval Division, Egypt, 21, Y

Bertie Connett, Able Seaman, 211894, 31/05/1916, *Indefatigable*, Jutland, 34, Y

Thomas John Connett, Boy 2nd Class, J/79472, 25/11/1917, Home, Died of Pneumonia, 15, N

Edwin Coombes, Stoker 1st Class, 305945, 06/08/1914, *Amphion*, Sunk by Mine, 33, Y

Charles Coombs, Petty Officer Stoker, 296640, 08/02/1915, Torpedo Boat 1, N/A, 36, Y

Abraham Cooper, Stoker 1st Class, 205696, 13/05/1915, *Goliath*, Gallipoli, 31, Y

Tom Disraeli Cross, Petty Officer, 210488, 31/05/1916, *Invincible*, Jutland, 32, N

George Edward Cumming, Lieutenant Commander, N/A, 01/11/1914, *Good Hope*, Coronel, 29, Y

Stewart Briscoe Dundee-Hooper, Lieutenant, N/A, 15/08/1916, Submarine E4, Collided with E41, 25, Y

Walter Eden, Stoker 1st Class, K/4379, 26/11/1914, Bulwark, Accidental Explosion, 22, N

William George Edwards, Able Seaman, R/484, 27/12/1917, Nelson Battalion Royal Naval Division, Western Front, 19, Y

Ernest George Sidney Fey, Chief Stoker, 276910, 31/05/1916, *Indefatigable*, Jutland, 43, Y

William John Wall Fletcher, Lieutenant, N/A, 31/05/1916, *Black Prince*, Jutland, 33, Y

George French, Petty Officer 1st Class, 168030, 01/12/1914, Berwick, N/A, 38, N

George German, Able Seaman, 185600, 25/05/1915, *Triumph*, Sunk by U-21, 35, Y

W.H. Hammett, Officer's Servant, Unknown, 31/05/1916, Unknown, Jutland, 19, N

Samuel Hannaford, Able Seaman, 199233, 04/02/1916, Moorsom, Accidental Drowning, 33, Y

Samuel Harding, Leading Stoker, 280105, 13/05/1915, *Goliath*, Gallipoli, 41, Y
Richard Thomas Harris, Able Seaman, 224639, 01/11/1914, *Monmouth*, Coronel, 28, Y
Arthur Leyland Harrison, Lieutenant-Commander, N/A, 23/04/1918, *Vindictive*, Zeebrugge Raid, 32, N
Frank William Edwin Hawke, Telegraphist, J/17608, 31/05/1916, *Defence*, Jutland, 19, Y
John Pain Hellings, Ship's Corporal 1st Class, 167553, 01/11/1914, Monmouth, Coronel, 38, Y
Charles Hewett, Leading Seaman, 234444, 13/05/1915, *Goliath*, Gallipoli, 27, Y
? Holmes, Seaman, 31/05/1916, *Queen Mary*, Jutland, Unknown, N
Harry Hooper, Able Seaman, J/1443, 31/08/1916, Gibraltar, N/A, 24, Y
W.G. Hutchings, Unknown, Unknown, 01/11/1914, *Monmouth*, Coronel, Unknown, N
William John Hutchings, Able Seaman, 224640, 31/05/1916, *Broke*, Jutland, 29, Y
Henry Isaac, Stoker Petty Officer, 358211, 30/09/1918, *Seagull*, Sunk in Collision, 27, Y
James Jarvis, Private, PLY/160702, 01/11/1914, *Monmouth*, Coronel, 20, Y
George Hearn Jenkins, Able Seaman, 179411, 31/05/1916, *Indefatigable*, Jutland, 39, Y
F. Johnson, Petty Officer, Unknown, c. August 1917, Unknown, N/A, 27, Y
Henry Jones, Stoker 1st Class, 293395, 13/05/1915, *Goliath*, Gallipoli, 43, Y
John Lewis, Able Seaman, 218282, 02/03/1918, Submarine H5, Rammed by Rutherglen, 32, Y
Frederick William Lintern, Stoker 1st Class, 304063, 31/05/1916, *Queen Mary*, Jutland, 33, N
Henry John Lock, Lieutenant, N/A, 26/11/1914, Bulwark, N/A, N
Sidney William Loddey, Petty Officer 1st Class, 203282, 25/01/1917, SS *Laurentic*, Sunk by Mine, 34, Y
Horace Martin, Able Seaman, R/218, 04/11/1917, Drake Battalion Royal Navy Division, Passchendaele, 20, Y
Thomas McIver, Corporal, PLY/8902, 13/11/1916, 1st Royal Marine Battalion, Royal Naval Division, Western Front, 37, Y
Thomas Lawton Mellor, Leading Seaman, J/4502, 31/05/1916, *Indefatigable*, Jutland, 22, Y
John Penn Milton, Midshipman, Unknown, 09/07/1917, *Vanguard*, Explosion in dock, Unknown, Y
William Walter Frederick Newland, Mechanician, 358523, 01/11/1914, *Monmouth*, Coronel, 28, Y
William Albert Nightingale, Officer's Steward 3rd Class, L/8376, 07/04/1916, *Victory*, N/A, 23, N
Arthur George Norman, Chief Petty Officer, 229750, 31/05/1916, *Indefatigable*, Jutland, 28, Y
Henry Northway, 1st Class Stoker, 166772, 13/05/1915, *Goliath*, Gallipoli, 38, Y
George William Peake, Stoker 2nd Class, K/29056, 31/05/1916, *Defence*, Jutland, 25, N

Thomas Edgar Prowse, Leading Seaman, 236024, 31/05/1916, *Defence*, Jutland, 28, Y

William Puzey, Leading Stoker, K/8182, 21/10/1917, *Marmion*, Collided with Tirade, 26, N

Arthur George Rendell, Leading Stoker, 311720, 31/05/1916, *Defence*, Jutland, 26, Y

? Rice, Able Seaman, 31/05/1916, *Queen Mary*, Jutland, Unknown, N

Percy John Saunders, Officer's Cook 2nd Class, L/1438, 01/11/1914, *Monmouth*, Coronel, 31, N

Frederick Scott, Leading Stoker, Unknown, 31/05/1916, *Queen Mary*, Jutland, Unknown, Y

William Edwin Shute, Able Seaman, R/2511, 05/11/1917, Hood Battalion Royal Naval Division, Passchendaele, 22, Y

Fred Skinner, Unknown, Unknown, 31/05/1916, *Defence*, Jutland, Unknown, N

James Smallbridge Short, Chief Petty Officer, 186518, 31/05/1916, *Indefatigable*, Jutland, 38, N

Richard John Stacey, Officer's Cook 2nd Class, L/1597, 01/11/1914, *Good Hope*, Coronel, 23, Y

Charles Ernest Samuel Steer, Able Seaman, 159703, 01/11/1914, *Monmouth*, Coronel, 39, Y

Alfred William Stephens, Chief Electrical Artificer 2nd Class, 347457, 31/05/1916, *Lion*, Jutland, 30, Y

William Edward Stroud, Shipwright 2nd Class, 115268, 22/09/1914, *Cressy*, Sunk by U-9, 54, Y

William Thorne, Stoker 1st Class, SS/100100, 13/05/1915, *Goliath*, Gallipoli, 27, N

Joseph Treby, Able Seaman, 199232, 01/11/1914, *Monmouth*, Coronel, 31, Y

? Trivian, Artificer Engineer, 31/05/1916, *Defence*, Jutland, Unknown, N

Arthur Walling, Private, PLY/10222, 30/04/1918, 4th Royal Marine Battalion, Home, 32, Y

James Albert Warring, Petty Officer Stoker, 288243, 11/02/1916, *Arabis*, Sunk off Dogger Bank, 36, Y

William Weeks, Leading Stoker, 280130, 13/05/1915, *Goliath*, Gallipoli, 44, Y

Stanley Westwater, Able Seaman, R/2730, 02/01/1918, Hood Battalion – Royal Naval Division, Western Front, 31, N

George Victor White, Officer's Steward 1st Class, 358692, 05/06/1916, *Hampshire*, Sunk by mine, 34, Y

Percy James White, Boy 1st Class, J/34034, 23/02/1915, *Impregnable*, N/A, 15, Y

Thomas William White, Private, PLY/8626, 07/11/1914, Royal Marines Light Infantry, N/A, 35, Y

Thomas Williams, Leading Wireless Telegraphist, Unknown, 31/05/1916, *Indefatigable*, Jutland, Unknown, N

Henry Windeatt, Petty Officer, 180405, 01/11/1914, Monmouth, Coronel, 37, Y

Reginald John Wood, Able Seaman, J/10565, 31/05/1916, *Indefatigable*, Jutland, 21, N

William Thomas Woodrow (or Woodward), Petty Officer, 197087, 31/05/1916, *Defence*, Jutland, 35, N

Statistics

Casualties by Year

Casualties By Year	Army	Navy	RAFC/RAF	Combined
1914	20	18	0	38
1915	61	12	0	73
1916	107	36	0	143
1917	178	12	0	190
1918	139	7	4	150
Total	**505**	**85**	**4**	**594**

Cause of Death amongst Infantry

Cause of Death	Number of Deaths
Killed in Action	294
Died of Wounds	107
Other (Illness and Wounds at Home)	98
At Sea	5
Accidently Killed	1
Total	**505**

Average Age of Casualties

	Army	Navy	Airforce	Combined
Average Age of Killed Soldier in 1914	27.14	32.40	N/A	29.77
Average Age of Killed Soldier in 1915	26.89	33.42	N/A	30.16
Average Age of Killed Soldier in 1916	27.99	28.47	N/A	28.23
Average Age of Killed Soldier in 1917	27.33	24.73	N/A	26.03
Average Age of Killed Soldier in 1918	26.93	31.43	20.75	26.37
Total	**27.26**	**30.09**	**20.75**	**28.11**

Torquay's Ten Bloodiest Days of the War

Battle	Number of Deaths
Battle of Jutland	29
Battle of the Somme (First Day)	15
Battle of Coronel	11
Battle of Loos (First Day)	9
Battle of Broodseinde	8
2nd Battle of Passchendaele (First Day)	8
HMS *Goliath* (Gallipoli Campaign)	8
Operation Michael (First Day)	6
Battle of Flers-Courcelette (First Day)	5
Battle of Langemarck (First Day)	4

Ten Worst Offensives for Torquay

Battle Killed in	Number of Deaths
Battle of the Somme	69
Battle of Passchendaele	57
Kaiserschlacht	49
Hundred Days	40
Battle of Arras	21
1914 Campaign	15
Battle of Loos	13
Mesopotamian Campaign	12
2nd Battle of Ypres	9
Battle of Cambrai	7

Regiments with the Greatest Number of Torquinian Casualties

Regiment/Corps	Number of Dead
Devonshire Regiment	159
Royal Engineers	34
Royal Field Artillery	22
Canadian Expeditionary Force	19
London Regiment	18
Somerset Light Infantry	17
Royal Fusiliers	15
Worcestershire Regiment	13
Royal Army Service Corps	13
Royal Army Medical Corps	11

Bibliography

Primary Sources

Christie, Agatha, *Agatha Christie: An Autobiography* (Collins, London, 1977)

Cliff, Norman D., *To Hell and Back with the Guards* (Merlin Books Ltd., Braunton, 1988)

Soldiers Died in the Great War: 1914-1919

The London Gazette

The Times

Torbay News and Dartmouth Gazette TN

Torquay Directory and South Devon Journal TD

Torquay Times TT

Torquay Town Council Minutes 1914-1920 (Torquay Public Library) (Multiple Volumes)

WO/363 British Army World War One Service Records

WO/364 British Army World War One Pension Records

Secondary Sources

Aggett, W.J.P, *The Bloody Eleventh: History of the Devonshire Regiment: Volume III: 1914-1969* (Tony Lee Ltd., Exeter, 1995)

Arthur, Max, *We Will Remember Them: Voices from the Aftermath of the Great War* (Weidenfeld & Nicolson, London, 2009)

Atkinson, C.T, *The Devonshire Regiment: 1914-1918* (Simpkin, Marshall, Hamilton, Kent & Co. Ltd, 1926)

Batten, Raymond C., *A Torquay Athletic R.F.C. History* (Kingfisher Print and Design Ltd., Totnes, 2002)

Bilton, David, *The Home Front in the Great War: Aspects of the Conflict 1914-1918* (Pen & Sword Books Ltd., Barnsley, 2003)

Burk, Kathleen, *Old World, New World: The Story of Britain and America* (Abacus, London, 2009)

Colwill, Reginald A., *Through Hell to Victory: From Passchendaele to Mons with the 2nd Devons in 1918* (Naval and Military Press Ltd., Uckfield, 2001) (Reprint of original, Torquay, 1927)

Drew, Lieutenant H.T.B, *The War Effort of New Zealand* (Whitcombe and Tombs Ltd., Auckland, 1923)

Duff, Michael et al., *The New Maritime History of Devon: Volume II: From the Late Eighteenth Century to the Present Day* (Conway Maritime Press, London, 1994)

Edwards, Leigh, *Torquay United: The Official Centenary History: 1899-1999* (Bookcraft, Bath, 1999)

Ferguson, Niall, *The Pity of War: 1914-1918* (Penguin Books, London, 1999)

French, David, *Spy Fever in Britain: 1900-1915 in The Historical Journal,* Vol. 21, No.2 (June 1978) pp.355-370

Grann, David, *The Lost City of Z: A Legendary British Explorer's Deadly Quest to Uncover the Secrets of the Amazon* (Pocket Books, London, 2010)

Gray, Todd, *Blackshirts in Devon* (The Mint Press, Exeter, 2006)

Gray, Todd, *Lest Devon Forgets* (The Mint Press, Exeter, 2010)

Gregory, Adrian, *The Last Great War: British Society and the First World War* (Cambridge University Press, Cambridge, 2008)

Griffith, Paddy, *Battle Tactics of the Western Front: The British Army's Art of Attack 1916-18* (Yale University Press, New Haven & London, 1994)

Gudmundsson, Bruce, *The British Expeditionary Force 1914-15* (Osprey Publishing, Oxford, 2005)

Hart, Peter, *1918: A Very British Victory* (Weidenfeld & Nicolson, London, 2008)

Hogarty, Patrick, *A Brief History of 'The Blue Caps' – The 1st Battalion Royal Dublin Fusiliers: 1914-1922* (Self Published, 2005)

Kneil, William F., *Upton: A Travel Through Time: Volume II* (Riviera Press, Torquay, 2011)

Lethbridge, Henry James, *Torquay & Paignton: The Making of a Modern Resort* (Phillimore & Co Ltd., Chichester, 2003) p.156

Lloyd, Nick, *'With Faith and Without Fear': Sir Douglas Haig's Command of First Army during 1915 in The Journal of Military History*, Vol. 71, No. 4 (Oct., 2007), pp. 1051-1076

Massie, Robert K., *Castles of Steel: Britain, Germany and the Winning of the Great War at Sea* (Pimlico, London, 2005)

Oppitz, Leslie, *Tramways Remembered: West and South West England* (Countryside Books, Newbury, 1990)

Pennell, Catriona, *A Kingdom United: Popular Responses to the Outbreak of the First World War in Britain and Ireland* (Oxford University Press, Oxford, 2012)

Pike, J.R, *Torbay's Heritage: Torquay* (Torbay Borough Council, Torbay, 1994)

Pike, John, *Torquay: The Place and the People* (Devonshire Press, Torquay, 1992)

Powell, Geoffrey, *Plumer: The Soldier's General* (Pen and Sword Books Ltd., 2004)

Prince, Stephen, *The Blocking of Zeebrugge: Operation Z-O 1998* (Osprey Publishing, Oxford, 2010)

Saunders, Tim, *West Country Regiments on the Somme* (Pen and Sword Books Ltd., Barnsley, 2004)

Sheffield, Gary, *Forgotten Victory: The First World War: Myths and Realities* (Headline Book Publishing, London, 2002)

Sheffield, Gary and Todman, Dan (ed.), *Command and Control on the Western Front: The British Army's Experience 1914-1918* (Spellmount Limited, Stroud, 2007)

Simkins, Peter, *Kitchener's Army: The Raising of the New Armies 1914-1916* (Pen and Sword Books Ltd., Barnsley, 2007)

Stevenson, David, *1914-1918: The History of the First World War* (Penguin Books, London, 2005)

Stone, Norman, *The Eastern Front: 1914-17* (Penguin Books, London, 1998)

Terraine, John, *The Road to Passchendaele* (Leo Cooper Ltd., London, 1984)

Thompson, Mark, *The White War: Life and Death on the Italian Front 1915-1919* (Faber and Faber Limited, London, 2009)

Todman, Dan, *The Great War: Myth and Memory* (Bloomsbury, London, 2007)

Wasley, Gerald, *Devon in the Great War: 1914-1918* (Devon Books, Tiverton, 2000)

White, Bonnie J., 'Volunteerism and Early Recruitment Efforts in Devonshire, August 1914-December 1915' in *The Historical Journal*, 52, 3 (2009) pp.641-666

Websites

Library and Archives Canada (http://www.collectionscanada.gc.ca)

The Canadian Great War Project (http://www.canadiangreatwarproject.com/index.asp)

The Long, Long Trail (http://www.1914-1918.net/)

Mapping Our Anzacs (http://mappingouranzacs.naa.gov.au/)

The Australian War Memorial (http://www.awm.gov.au/)

Veterans Affairs Canada (http://www.veterans.gc.ca/eng/)

Index